DEMCO

What's a Mother To Do?

What's a Mother To Do?

Conversations on Work & Family

Michele Hoffnung

Trilogy Books
Pasadena, California

Publisher's Cataloging in Publication

Hoffnung, Michele, 1944 –
What's a mother to do: conversations on work and family / Michele Hoffnung.
p. cm.
Includes bibliographical references and index.
ISBN 0-9623879-1-6

1. Working mothers—United States. 2. Family—United States. I. Title.

HQ759.48.H6 1992   306.874
                                                 QBI921 18

Library of Congress Catalog Card Number: 91-68029
ISBN 0-9623879-1-6

To John Mack Faragher
For What We Share

Table of Contents

Preface and Acknowledgments

I am a mother, a wife, a college professor. For more than twenty years I have balanced the responsibilities of my family and my career. With the benefit of a job that has flexible hours, a spouse who shares home responsibilities, and relatives and friends who help, I have managed to raise wonderful children, earn a living, accomplish many of my work goals, and still maintain my sanity. Yet, when female students ask how I manage to "do it all," I know full well that I have not. There were years when I could do no original research or writing. There were long stretches when I had no time for myself. There is much I look forward to doing when my children are on their own, although I like them so much I am in no hurry for them to be grown. Being their mother has given meaning to my life, but it has also limited my range of accomplishments.

Like many young girls growing up in the fifties, I never even considered the option of a child-free life. I always knew I wanted to be a mother; my dreams were filled with babies, many babies. When I occasionally worried about having children, my concern was biological — would I be able to become pregnant? I decided early in life that I would adopt if my body failed me.

At the same time, I never doubted that I would go to college. I did not have any firm notion of what I would be when I finished college, but I felt lucky that I could be whatever I wanted. I did not feel the pressure to be a doctor, or at least a dentist, that I know my older brother felt. Because I was a girl, I would not have to support a family, so I could be anything.

My first career decision was to become a high school English teacher. My parents approved. My mother was an elementary school teacher so I was choosing to be like her, but not exactly. I majored in psychology, minored in English, and planned to take the necessary education courses for certification. In my senior year of college, encouraged by my academic success, I changed my mind. I applied to graduate schools in psychology and was accepted. Instead of practice teaching, I prepared to enter a doctoral program at the University of Michigan. Suddenly I was aware of having disappointed my father. In his mind public school teaching was the perfect job for a woman, one she could leave and reenter, one she could always fall back on. A Ph.D., he informed me, was too much education for a woman. Since I was determined to go to graduate school, he urged me to stop with a master's degree.

I did not consider the potential conflict between being a wife and mother and being a psychology professor. My father's warning that I would make myself unmarriageable fell on deaf ears. My brother had already given up medical science for psychology and I saw no reason why my professional choices should be limited by my gender. And I certainly never changed my commitment to becoming a mother. If no one would marry me, I rationalized, I could eventually have a baby on my own.

Before long, in spite of my father's fears, I was balancing the conflicting demands of career and motherhood. During my second year in graduate school I married a man eleven years my senior who had two children. Though his sons lived with their mother, he was an involved father. In spite of the fact that we were in Ann Arbor, Michigan, and they were in Chicago, we visited with them every other weekend and they lived with us for much of their non-school time. His age and our involvement with his boys combined with my strong desire for children and led us to start a family right away. My first son was born in June of my third year of graduate school.

I never considered not working. I thought having a baby during graduate school would be easier than when I was starting a new job, and I am sure I was right. I did not want to wait to become a mother until I had established myself in my career, although that is what I usually advise young women today. I started my first job as an assistant professor when my son was fourteen months old. I taught three days a week, was with the baby four days a week, and wrote lectures, graded papers, and edited my first book during nap times and evenings, often working well into the night. By mid-year I was a physical wreck. Luckily I was able to rest and recuperate during intersession and return to work in better shape for second semester. What, I have often asked myself, would have happened to me if I had had a profession that did not have intersessions, or three-day-a-week teaching schedules? What if my spouse had not also been a college professor who could arrange his schedule to complement mine, or had not been willing to share childcare?

Questions like these are what motivated this book. My story is but one particular variation on the theme of balancing employment and motherhood. My situation was difficult but not impossible. I had hard times but lots of rewards as well. I wanted to find out from other women how they manage the complicated choices about employment and motherhood. At a time when, more than ever before, women have control over their fertility as well as the opportunity to work outside the home, how do they make decisions about whether to have children and when to have children, whether to have careers and when to have careers, whether to stay home or to continue employment? And how much do their decisions actually affect their day-to-day lives?

It was three years later that I gave birth to my second son. My older son was in cooperative daycare; the baby came to work with me. I had a bassinet in my office; colleagues watched the baby while I was in class or at a meeting. Like all nursing mothers I was exhausted all the time, but with my second baby I was an experienced mother and teacher. I had learned a lot in three years of employed motherhood, enough so that I just expected to teach my classes and tend my children; I did not expect to do research and writing during that year. I had learned that if I wanted the joy of another baby I had to give up the fast track to professional recognition.

My research productivity picked up slowly once my children were out of infancy. Still, it is no accident that I finally found time to pursue my questions about motherhood well after my youngest child was in school. By then divorce and the creation of a new blended family had made me mother of three, including a stepdaughter between my two sons in age. Until that time I was too busy with the demands of motherhood and employment to study them systematically! Cooperative daycare required parent turns and parent meetings. Kindergarten required picking up midday and providing childcare in the afternoon. Even school days required afterschool supervision and care on sick days and snow days and holidays, but that still left me some private time, which felt like a lot compared to the demands of pre-school care.

While having children slowed down my career, it also enriched my professional interests. More than my extensive schooling (perhaps in spite of it), my experiences as a mother connected me with critical issues in women's lives. I thank Josh, Sarah, and Jesse for inadvertently raising the questions that motivated this book. I thank them also for believing that in addition to being their mother I could do anything else I set out to do.

As I ventured into this project I received assistance from several sources. I wish to thank the Quinnipiac College Faculty Research Committee for its continuing support in the forms of research funds and reduced teaching loads. Members of the Anna Wilder Phelps Social Science Seminar of the Wellesley College Center for Research on Women: Laurie Crumpacker, Kay Dunn, Ruth Harriet Jacobs, Frinde Maher, Diane Margolis, Robin Roth, Jane Torrey, Eleanor Vander Haegen, and Mary Roth Walsh, provided intellectual support for my early ideas about this book and read and commented on an early draft of a chapter. I thank them for their thoughtful reactions which helped me reconceptualize the book, as well as for their continuing encouragement. I also thank Peggy McIntosh for obtaining the funding and creating the Mellon program that brought that group of faculty women together. Parts of chapter one appeared in a slightly different form in the essay, "Motherhood: Contemporary Conflict for Women" in Jo Freeman's *Women: A Feminist Perspective*, 1984 and 1989.

I also wish to thank the individuals who have assisted me along the way. Ellen Greenhouse and Rachel Ranis were helpful consultants as I prepared to do the interviews. Susan Carter Elliott listened to all the taped interviews and made independent assessments of the women's experiences. She also listened to my endless talk about the project and read several drafts of several chapters. Susan's enthusiasm for the project, and love and encouragement for me as I obsessed with it, have been invaluable. Pearl Brown, Caltha Crowe, Steve Elliott, and Kathryn Marshall read and commented on early versions of several chapters. Emily Stier Adler, John Mack Faragher, Ellen Greenhouse, and Robin Roth generously took the time to read and comment on my entire manuscript. Their criticism has improved the book immensely. Marge Wood of Trilogy Books made valuable suggestions both large and small.

This book would not have been possible without the participation of the thirty women who opened up their homes and their lives to me. I am grateful to each of them for sharing their pain as well as their joy, for teaching me about themselves, and myself as a result.

Most of all, I wish to thank Johnny. As husband/lover/co-parent/friend he has helped to shape my life and my vision. He has been my chief supporter and critic throughout the long process of researching and writing; willing, in spite of his own demanding schedule, to listen to my problems, read drafts of my manuscript, and keep me one step ahead of my word processor. His contribution to my work and to my life is beyond measure. For these reasons, and more, it is to him that I dedicate this book.

1

Changing Ideas About Motherhood

Motherhood has a special position in the lives of women today; it brings with it both enormous benefits and enormous burdens. Bearing and raising children is essential work, necessary for the continuation of society, satisfying to human generative impulses, and highly valued in the lives of mothers. At the same time, it is undervalued by society and conflicts with other important aspects of women's lives — employment, economic independence, and egalitarian marriage. Mothering is done at home, outside the world of achievement, power, and money. It consequently pulls women who mother away from productive work for at least part of their adult lives.

This has not always been true. Recent work by social historians indicates that our modern notion of motherhood has its roots in the nineteenth century, when mothering became the highly exalted function of females to care for their children and impart to them the highest spiritual values.[1] Prior to this glorification of motherhood by the nineteenth-century middle class, the bearing and rearing of children was integrated into the other work women did and was not women's most important work. In a subsistence farm economy, survival required women as well as men place productive work before reproductive concerns. Women and men worked side by side, in and around the home. Women were responsible for food and clothing production for the family, which involved many complicated skills, as well as for cooking, laundering, cleaning, and childcare.[2] Infants were tended when possible, and were sometimes played with, but were never the center of their mother's attention. Their care was largely the task of older siblings. Those children who survived infancy quickly took their places in the social and economic life of the family.[3]

Industrialization simultaneously disrupted the unity of home and workshop, decreased patriarchal power, and devalued women's work within the family. Life in industrial society is characterized by distinct separations: work from play, production from reproduction, adulthood from childhood. Adults work, children play. Work takes place in the office or factory, relaxation in the home. Activities done outside the home are reimbursed with money; inside the home, activities are done for love. Within this new set of values, which emerged during the nineteenth century, women were assigned to the home as nonproducing homemakers. In this context, mother-work became the focus of their attention. As work transformed into wage labor in factory or office, the family took on new meaning. It became a refuge, the place to which dad and kids came to recover from the pressure and pain of alienated work and school.[4] The burden of providing the comforts of home was assigned to women.

The combination of homemaking and childcare is a full-time job, but it carries none of the economic benefits that employment outside the home provides. Although these reproductive tasks were more physically demanding in days gone by, they were not severed from the productive work of the family or imbued with heavy psychological significance. In contrast to the economic value of women's work in the past, today a woman's devotion to "women's work" makes her dependent on the people she tends. It results in an economic dependence on her husband — a man chosen for love — and a psychological dependence on her children as products of her mothering.

We all know that the work women do in the home is valuable. It is scary to imagine life without it: dirty floors, dirty clothes, empty refrigerators, wet and hungry babies, and so on. The problem is that in spite of its human value, such work brings no money, no status, no prestige. A woman who devotes herself entirely to family work ends up apologizing that she is "just a housewife." One who is employed in addition ends up with two jobs and one paycheck, a paycheck that is likely to be smaller than her male counterpart's because he is likely to have a wife to care for his home and children, enabling him to devote full energy to his work.

Other historic changes have made more choices possible for women. Prior to the nineteenth century, abstinence was the only effective method of controlling fertility.[5] Technological improvements and political struggles have made contraception relatively safe, effective, and available in the twentieth century. With the repeal of restrictive birth control legislation in the 1960s, heterosexual intimacy is no longer inseparable from maternity. This leaves contemporary women with more choices than ever before.

Most women want to be mothers and most mothers want at least two children, but many do not want to stop working outside the home and many must work to support their families.[6] As a result they control, to a large extent, the rate and timing of their childbearing in order to lessen its demands and maintain their other commitments. In our country the birth rate has decreased steadily since the nineteenth century;[7] in the last three decades alone, the fertility rate of American women has fallen nearly 50 percent.[8] Women have made a dramatic choice to have fewer children, to end their childbearing earlier, or to start their families later. This steady decrease in the number of births per woman reflects more than the availability of contraception. It also reflects a perception on the part of increasing numbers of women that life has exciting and rewarding experiences to offer in addition to childbearing and that these are within their reach.

American women's participation in the labor force has increased steadily since 1900; gradually until 1940, more rapidly since then. In 1900 only 20 percent of all women of working age (16-64 were in the paid labor force. By 1980, 52 percent of women aged 16-64 worked.[9] Not only has there been a change in the number of women in the work force, but there has been a dramatic shift in the pattern of employment in women's life cycle. In 1900, the highest proportion of female workers were young, single women. If a woman worked it would be before marriage; very few worked later in life. Although this pattern was still true in 1940, the number of women working was higher. By 1950, however, while young, single women continued to work, married women in their late thirties had begun to return to the labor force. For the first time, employment rates for women 40-44 years old exceeded those for women 25-29. By 1960, the trend was so pronounced that the highest labor force participation rate for women was among 45-49-year-olds. The greatest increase since 1940 has been for married women living with their husbands.[10] In recent years this trend for married women to be in the labor force has expanded to include women with children, even women with preschool children. In 1988, 53 percent of mothers with children under three were in the labor force, and 51 percent of mothers with infants under one were in the labor force. Of the mothers of preschoolers who were not employed, 25 percent said they would choose to work if safe and affordable childcare were available.[11] For a variety of reasons, more than half the mothers with preschoolers are employed.

As I look at the lives of the women around me — friends, relatives, and colleagues of about my age — I am impressed by the range of choices these women have made in the timing of childbearing. A best friend about my own age gave birth to her first child just weeks after my oldest reached majority. A few of my friends have children older than mine, a few are now trying to start families, and others fall everywhere in between. Almost all have careers as well. My acquaintances do not represent contemporary women in general, but their various decisions regarding childbearing are an indication of women's changing options.

As my personal experience illustrates, there are two sets of expectations for contemporary women. We are expected to be individuals who achieve in school and prepare to take our equal places in the world of work. We are also expected to want husbands and babies and to take primary responsibility for family life.[12] Although these expectations conflict, the conflict is not always acute. Most girls learn to compartmentalize, to keep separate the feelings associated with achievement from those associated with femininity, and to handle them as mutually exclusive.[13] Separation is one strategy for coping with essentially contradictory expectations.[14] Indeed, the very structure of modern life makes this distinction appear "natural." Girls achieve in school; then, at home, as daughters and sisters, they assist in women's caretaking roles.

Although family responsibilities fall disproportionately on daughters rather than sons, and wives rather than husbands, to a large extent women can meet these responsibilities and still strive for individual success in the world outside the family. Schoolgirls can do the dishes as well as their homework even though their brothers are not expected to. Wives can make dinner after a day of work even though their husbands sit down and watch the news. Through school, during the early years on a job, or in a childless marriage, middle-class women may notice contradictions, feel anger at sex discrimination at work or unequal responsibility for housework, or feel guilt about their shortcomings; but to a large extent they can manage to fulfill both sets of expectations. It is the birth of the first child that provides the strong push to stay home and typically brings abrupt and complete change in the new mother's life activities.[15]

Women assume primary responsibility for infant and child care. Even mothers who are employed make the arrangements for childcare while they are out of the home and do the primary care when they are home. Women do this in part because it has traditionally been expected of them. They also do it because early in life they develop a connected sense of self, a sense of interdependence in relation to others that makes the activity of caring for others' needs vital to their own well-being. Women feel connected to their children, and to other family members as well, and typically do not envision their own development separate from that relational context. While young boys too develop this ethic of care, they are more likely to learn to give it up in their quest for a masculine identity which stresses autonomy in relation to others.[16] Women, as a result, are the ones who typically limit their commitment at work so that they can be mothers as well as workers.

While men traditionally have been expected to devote themselves to achieving in the work world, with marriage and family as secondary, women are encouraged to achieve but also expected to bear and care for children. Consequently, although almost all men start work when they leave school and continue employment until retirement, few women follow that pattern. Louise Kapp Howe has identified three major employment patterns that women follow after leaving school.[17] The first is to work for a few years and then give up employment to become a homemaker. This used to be the dominant pattern. The second is to follow the same pattern as men, to begin work after leaving school and continue until retirement. This pattern is most frequent among women who have no children, black women, and professional and managerial women. A growing percentage of young women (those born after 1944) are joining the work force with the steady, long-term, full-time commitment that fits this pattern.[18] The third pattern is to work until having children, take time off to raise them, and then return to work. The time off for full-time mothering used to be 5-10 years, but the interval has been getting shorter. This is the pattern that has grown fastest during this century.

More women are working than ever before and working for a substantially greater proportion of their adult lives. Most women still choose to be mothers, but this no longer means they will not be workers. How do they do it?

I began this study because I was interested in how women made their choices about work and family and how they managed the competing demands. I read everything that was written about the topic but all I learned was how women were supposed to feel, what women were supposed to do, and what was supposed to be good for children. Those ideas did not fit with my experience and did not tell me about other women's experiences. I spoke with scores of women about their childbearing choices and conflicts. I talked to friends, family, and acquaintances. I talked to women in my classes, at talks I gave at area libraries, and in the various places I would meet them.

These informal conversations prepared me for the formal inter-views that are the basis for this book. I conducted in-depth interviews with thirty mothers of at least one preschool-age child. I selected the preschool years because it is then that total responsibility for childcare resides within the family, most often with the mother. These are, therefore, the most active mothering years. I selected white, middle-class women living within an area of southern Connecticut because this particular location is populated by both long-established, local families and profes-sional, mobile families attracted by its proximity to New Haven.[19]

The number thirty is both small and large. It is too small to make empirical generalizations about all mothers. My inten-tion, however, was to understand the quality of these individual women's lives. This required spending many hours with each woman. I visited each in her home at least twice, spent from four to ten hours with her — chatting, listening to anecdotes, waiting for infants to be quieted, phones to be answered, children's problems to be solved. The interviews took the form of extensive conversations about their experiences and feelings as women and mothers. All the interviews were taped and later transcribed. For a qualitative study of this type the sample was large.[20]

In the chapters that follow women tell about many aspects of their lives. In order to condense many hours of conversation I have selected from and reorganized the many things they told me. My goal was to make their stories clear in their own terms but, since I asked the questions and did the editing, I helped shape each story.

Before we turn to the individual women and the choices they made, it is important to recognize that every woman does not have every choice equally available to her. While I, for example, never doubted that I would go to college, another woman may never have considered college, and a third may have wanted college but not had the financial backing to enable her to go. Previous research indicates that five areas of women's experience are important determinants of their available choices: socio-economic background, educational level, career orientation, employment history, and geographical proximity to extended family. (I have put details about these dimensions of the group in an appendix.)

The socio-economic level of a woman's family of origin strongly influences her life choices; women with working-class backgrounds have fewer attractive opportunities than women with middle-class backgrounds — less college, less travel, less living on their own. Middle-class families are likely to launch their daughters into the world by sending them to college, just as they do their sons. They do not expect their children to return home to live after college. In contrast, working-class families typically supervise their daughters very closely. They expect them to live at home until they marry, commuting to college if they attend. Marriage is the most acceptable way out of the parental home. Since when their mothers work outside the home it is at low-paying, tedious jobs, working-class girls lack models to follow of women employed in interesting and rewarding occupations so instead dream about love and marriage transforming their lives. Their lack of options and desire for freedom from their parents push them in the direction of early marriage.[21] Working-class girls, as a result, grow up faster than middle-class girls, without the luxury of an extended "prime time" between graduation from high school, the end of adolescence, and marriage, the beginning of adulthood.[22] Prime time is a time of options: college, vocational training, work, travel, cohabitation, marriage; but a long prime time is primarily reserved for those from affluent backgrounds.

Education is a major determinant of women's labor force participation; better educated women are more likely to be employed than less educated women, whether they are single or married, whether or not they are mothers. For women more than men, credentials are necessary to be considered for positions in the labor market. While it is still possible to be a "self-made man," it is essential for a woman to demonstrate that she is well-qualified and highly motivated. Opportunities for employment, therefore, increase as a function of educational level for women more than for men, as do the earnings given up if they do not work.[23] Since 1960 there has been a large movement into colleges of women from the middle and lower classes. Educational level as measured by the number of years in school, therefore, is fast becoming homogeneous among women. There are large status differences, however, in who goes to which institutions of higher education: in general, upper-middle-class women attend elite, private institutions and the public ivys; lower-middle-class women attend public colleges; and working-class women attend community colleges. These different types of schools provide different levels of education, from strictly vocational to training in the liberal arts, and result in employment prospects with different degrees of attractiveness.[24]

Career orientation refers to a woman's commitment to a profession, a position in the work force that requires specialized training. Although almost all college women expect to work at some time in their lives, almost all desire marriage and children and almost all stress the centrality of family life in their future plans.[25] One of the consequences of this is that they remain flexible in their career choices, far more flexible than men for whom career is the central choice. College women are more likely to be indecisive or to resort to the "women's" fields of nursing, elementary or secondary school teaching, social work, and library science, in order to reduce conflict between career and family.[26] They plan to participate in the labor force but their primary commitment is to family. While most mothers do hold jobs, many consider them secondary to their real work as mothers.

Women with career commitment, in contrast, are more likely to consider employment an integral aspect of their lives rather than something "to fall back on." They train for professions or careers just like their male counterparts and are committed to them in a life-long way, just as men are. Lydia O'Donnell refers to this commitment as "labor force involvement," in distinction to "labor force participation."[27] Increasingly, women born after 1944 are labor force involved like male workers.[28]

Employment for wives is associated with more power within the marriage than is full-time homemaking. Studies that have looked at decision making and role sharing between married couples have found greater equality between husband and wife when the wife is employed.[29] Studies of marital power show that the husband's power is greatest when the wife is not earning and is engaged in caring for a small child.[30] When the wife is employed the husband participates more in house and child care than when the wife is home, although he does not share the burden equally. Kathryn Walker found that husbands of working wives assisted one to three hours per day, while the wives spent four to eight hours on housework.[31] Joseph Pleck found that the full-time employed wife's share of the domestic tasks was three times as great as that of her full-time employed husband.[32] Nonetheless, husbands of employed wives do a higher percentage of the couple's total family work than do husbands of homemakers. Husbands in dual-income households do 30 to 35 percent; sole-earner husbands, 20 percent.[33]

Since women have primary responsibility for home and child care, the typical three-category system — full-time employed, part-time employed, unemployed — does not do justice to the quality of their working lives. The stereotyped images of either employed mother or homebound mother, for example, do not adequately describe the situations of the mothers with whom I have spoken. Quietly, one by one, they have devised a rich variety of employment schedules. While some are employed full time away from home and some are full-time mothers and homemakers, the majority are employed but arrange their work so they can be home for a large portion, even most, of their children's waking hours, much as I had done when my children were young. In most instances, however, this flexibility is accomplished by taking jobs that are convenient, rather than jobs that are challenging or lucrative.[34]

Living in close proximity to extended family is indicative of a close-knit family network. Closeness of kinship network is related to the degree of role segregation between husband and wife. The more closely knit the network, the more help the woman has from female kin and friends and the more complete the role segregation is between husband and wife.[35] Close family networks provide mothers with the advice, assistance, and companionship of their female kin, which establishes a social context that discourages help from husbands, and exerts pressure on women to accept traditional family roles. This makes it more difficult for the mother to devote herself to commitments outside the family.[36] Carol Stack found that, among the black urban poor she studied, female kin had an essential role in helping mother children; kin networks provided security in a situation of unending scarcity. At the same time, security in the networks worked "against successful marriage or long-term relationships" between women and men; bonds with female kin conflicted with nuclear family formation by draining time, energy, and economic resources.[37]

These five areas—socio-economic background, educational level, career orientation, employment history, and geographical proximity to extended family—represent large social forces that help shape women's lives and the choices they make about employment and motherhood. In the chapters that follow we will see how eight individual women respond to the expectations their families have for them and to the opportunities that come their way.

These forces, though important, are not the only elements that shape the life course. Some unpredictable events, divorce for example, or unexpected employment opportunities, add variety to women's experiences. Another factor has to do with planning. Helpful in most spheres of adult life, planning is particularly beneficial in the sphere of parenthood.[38] The motherhood mystique leads people to believe that having a child will automatically be a satisfying and fulfilling focus of a new mother's life. Rather, it is a stage of life with its own dilemmas, demands, joys, and pain.[39] Preparing for it, timing it, organizing one's life to encompass it, engaging social support for it, all contribute to making motherhood a positive experience. This element of planning, more than any other, shows up in the lives of the thirty women and in the chapters that follow.

The following chapters are devoted to intimate portrayals of eight of these women. I have changed their names in order to protect their privacy, but their words and stories remain theirs. The individuals I have selected represent both mothers with career commitment and those without. Within each of those categories I have included two who are employed and two who are not. As a result, half of the mothers are doing what they had planned, working or full-time homemaking, the other half are not. Alice and Linda expected to be mothers and home-makers, and they are. Elizabeth and Nina planned to pursue careers in addition to being mothers, and they are employed. Ellen and Janet planned to be at home full time, but found that they needed to work. Pam and Amy planned to pursue careers, but ended up as full-time homemakers, working outside the home only a couple of hours a week. How these women work out the conflicting expectations of work and family, and how they feel about themselves, are the major questions of this book.

These eight individuals come from different social and eco-nomic backgrounds, have different levels of education and career commitment, different work histories, and live in differ-ent proximity to kin. By no means do they represent all mothers, but because their lives are similar to those of other mothers, their experiences can deepen our understanding of the impact of motherhood.

2

Alice

Kids lead you off in different directions.

Alice chose to be a homemaker. As a little girl she imagined being a nurse or a nun, but she always expected to be a wife and mother; she never wanted a career. Although by the time her husband finished medical school she had earned her master's degree and had enjoyed five years of full-time employment as a research biochemist, she still did not want to pursue a career. She stopped working and became a full-time wife, mother, and homemaker.

Her strong commitment to family life is rooted in her happy experiences growing up in a large, close-knit kinship network. Her mother serves as a model for her, and her parents' relationship as a model for her marriage. She and her husband have developed a traditional division of labor that meets her needs for family life and his for career advancement. This has encouraged the development of separate interests; as a result, they are not as close friends as they used to be.

Alice is a mother and homemaker without commitment to a career, who is not employed. Fourteen of the thirty women I spoke with clearly fit this category, and another four work so few hours a week that by any standard measure they too would be considered unemployed. Alice is also mobile, well-educated, and upper-middle class. There is no economic pressure to seek employment and, given her husband's commitment to his medical career, lots of need for her services at home.

She perceives motherhood as having had a strongly positive effect on her life. It pulled her away from employment and, as a result, gave her more freedom. It expanded her interests, taking her from the narrow focus of her scientific work to a broad involvement with the community. For Alice, this was an unexpected benefit of having children.

❦ ❦ ❦

I just assumed I would get married and I would have children and life would be rosy, much like my mother's. I loved babies when I was a child. I can remember being little, five or six, and having baby cousins. I absolutely adored babies when I was little.

I think marriage and motherhood was something you took for granted, at least in my generation. I don't think I separated the two. I'm sure my daughter does not feel that way at all. I think she's going to have a lot more problems because ultimately she will have many choices and I think that tends to make lots of people just wander aimlessly.

Alice grew up in the midwest, in a family of four. Her mother was a homemaker, her father worked in the post office, and she had a brother who was younger by two years. Her family was part of a close-knit working-class kinship network.

It was a very large family and close, particularly my mother's side of the family. For every holiday you all got together, and you always went to your grandfather's house for Father's Day, and that kind of stuff. And everybody brought over gifts — I think there were forty people. It was lots of fun. I miss that for my children now because we are separated from both of our families. I feel badly because I think they are missing a lot of inter-family activities that are a lot of fun.

Alice attended Catholic elementary and high school, then, following a working-class pattern, she remained at home and commuted to a local college, majoring in chemistry. Upon graduation from college she took a job in a lab and continued to live at home, paying her folks for room and board. Two years later, with the encouragement of her employer, she did the unexpected and went to graduate school in the northeast. There she earned her master's degree and met her husband, Brian. Alice and Brian married two years after they met, while he was still in school and she was employed as a biochemist. They lived in the city in which Brian had been raised, near his large, close-knit, extended Italian family.

> We were classmates and very good friends. It wasn't just a matter of we'll go out on Friday nights or anything, I mean we were just together all the time because we were in the same program. Then the time was right to get married. We were both ready. I think if we hadn't gotten married then we probably would have just drifted apart. I think relationships just reach a point where you either move on to something else or you can't go home again, that kind of thing.
>
> I was almost twenty-seven when I got married. For people my age, that was old. Most kids were getting married younger, right out of school. My parents didn't want me doing that, but then there were many people getting married about twenty-one or twenty-two. Lots of people I know would get pressure from their families. I don't ever really remember getting that at all, though I married fairly late.

When we spoke, Alice was thirty-nine years old; Brian was thirty-eight; their three children were ten, six, and five. Brian was a doctor, Alice a mother and homemaker. They owned their large, nicely furnished home.

For Alice and Brian, the decision to start a family was an easy one. Family life had always been important to each of them; they married because they wanted to start a family of their own.

> We had talked about having children before we were married and knew that we wanted a family. We both came from families in which there were only two children; we thought we wanted a large family. We knew we certainly wanted more than one child and probably more than two. We were just sort of ready.
>
> I knew I was going to work while he was in medical school; I knew that I was our support. One of us had to have an income and I knew, whether I had a child or not, that I was going to

have to work. Still, it was an extremely easy decision — there was no big hassle about it at all.

We both had a pretty strong sense of family and I think that's why we had children. This marriage was just not a you and I kind of thing; we were creating a family. I think that's why we got married, because we wanted a family; not necessarily that we wanted to have children, but we wanted to be a family and children become part of your family.

I wonder why married women who choose not to have children bother getting married. It seems to me that you don't really need to get married to have the same kind of relationship with another mature person that you do in a marriage. And I don't know why you would choose not to have children. I think a man and a woman can be a family, but I think family involves more than just two people. It involves the family that you left and also the children that you might have.

Andy, their first child, was born a year and a half after they married. Alice used birth control pills until they decided it was time to have a baby. Her pregnancy was easy.

I was not sick; I've never been morning sick. I had no problems. I knew I was going to go back to work; I didn't worry about it. I worry much more about money now, when obviously my husband is making a lot more money than I ever made. Money's just a much bigger hassle now than it ever was then. We just managed.

I sort of liked being pregnant. I did like being pregnant because he was the first grandchild in Brian's family; it was a very special thing. It was my parents' first grandchild, too, and that was a very special thing.

I worked until about two weeks before he was born, maybe three weeks or so before he was born, because at that point I was having lots of edema. The doctor said, "Now you are going to have to stay home," because he wasn't sure what was going on at that point. Then I stayed home and waited two weeks for him to be born. It was ridiculous.

I thought I was going to have natural childbirth. I remember I went through a whole bunch of natural childbirth classes and I think I was probably as aware as anybody else of specifically what was happening and what was going to happen. Probably a lot more attuned to the process than lots of people who have babies. So I wasn't scared or anything; I don't remember being scared. He was late and I can remember just thinking, "Where is this baby? When is it ever coming?" But I don't ever remember being afraid; even when I was in labor I was not afraid of anything. The one thing that I can remember is that when I went to the hospital to have him I was not in active labor at all and I was in this bed listening to somebody in another room moaning and groaning and I thought, "Oh, boy, if I have to do this for hours I probably will get hysterical." But that stopped, and then I just was there for a while.

When I had been in labor for twelve hours or so they said, "We don't know what's going on or how long you'll be." They kept taking me out and x-raying me because the baby was never engaging. He never engaged at all and they couldn't figure out what was going on. They could push his head down, but as soon as they stopped pushing it would come back up. I was in strong labor but I was not dilating and his head was not engaging and they said, "I think maybe you ought to have something to rest now. You've been doing this long enough." So I agreed — yes, I was getting kind of tired about the whole thing — and I was medicated then. I was really drugged. I did not know it was going to be a section until I went into the operating room; they had obviously gotten my husband's permission at that stage.

And then he was born — he was born by Cesarean section because there was some fetal distress after about fourteen hours of labor. I was so elated! I have never had such a high as after he was born! I guess it's the first child; you're so up for the whole thing. I think I could have flown if I had tried. I am quite sure I could have flown around the room. This was not the day he was born, because I was pretty sedated that day and I kept falling asleep, but the second day when I was aware of what happened — that now I had the baby. I have never felt that way about anything else at all: not getting married, not my other kids, nothing.[1]

The birth of the first child, often a dramatic turning point in a woman's life, was an easy transition for Alice, who had no choice but to continue her full-time employment. Knowing that she would be continuing employment, she had arranged for childcare help before the baby was born so felt relaxed and well-prepared.

When I was pregnant I had to make plans; childcare was a consideration and that worked out very easily. We were concerned that we find someone who was going to be adequate and loving and would be a good substitute, but there was no problem.

It was easy with the first sitter because we lived in this complex and there were a couple of other medical school families in the complex. This one girl was staying home with her daughter, who was maybe a year, a year and a half, and she knew I needed a babysitter and she offered to babysit for the child. And then, when she no longer did it, I had to look for someone else, and I put ads in the community newspaper and asked people if they knew anybody who wanted to babysit. The girl who I finally did get came through the newspaper ad. She was coming to the house — that's what was good about it.

Alice's childhood love for babies continued, making infant care an enjoyable experience.

I like babies a lot and I think they are super fun. I think there are some people who just like having babies, taking care of babies, having babies around. I like kids at that stage. I love finding them where you put them; you put them down and they're there when you go back. I think that's much nicer than "Where is this kid now and what is he getting into?" I love the warmth of picking up this little body.... I think babies are really sweet.

Although Alice would have preferred to stay home with her baby, she accepted that she would have to work while Brian was in school and enjoyed the work she did. On the day that she went back to work after Andy was born, however, she felt intense conflict.

The worst day of my life was the day I went back to work for the first time after my son was born. I had to work — I was the only support that we had. He was about two months old when I went back to work. I clearly remember taking him over to this other girl's apartment, which was just across the hall, walking down the hall, getting in the car, and driving to work crying the entire way. God! It was just horrible! It worked out fine, but the first day I thought, "If I get to work without killing myself it will be incredible!" I only cried that one day. I suppose I felt bad about it all the time; never intensely bad, but I felt bad about it the entire time.

I can remember one day — I guess it must have been a school vacation and my husband was home. The girl who sat for us was going to visit her family so my husband was going to take care of Andy. There was something else he wanted or had to do, and he resented very much that he was being left with the baby. I can remember crying just terribly about it. I didn't want him to have to stay with him; I would stay home and take care of him. I can remember feeling very badly about that. So, I suppose I felt badly about it the entire time, but I had to be realistic and do things I had to do. I really enjoyed working. I was doing the kind of thing I liked to do.

Although Alice was working full time and supporting the family, childcare was her responsibility. She and Brian replicated the traditional role assignments with which they had grown up in their childhood homes, only Alice worked in addition. Nonetheless, Alice actively chose her path and, in spite of feeling bad about having to leave her baby, enjoyed combining employment and motherhood. She did not want to wait two more years to have a child and had high enough earning power so she could hire substitute care. She also liked her job and knew her husband would make enough to support them after he finished school. Alice chose to stop working when her income was no longer necessary, about two years after Andy was born.

Alice breastfed all of her children.

The first one for about five months, the second one for about five months, and the third one longer, maybe nine or ten months. He went right to the cup. The first one I was working, and so breastfeeding was starting to be a problem. He was having bottles and breast and that just sort of tapered off into only bottles. When I was breastfeeding the second one I got pregnant, and so that was a good time to stop.

Alice's first pregnancy was easy; she needed no outside help.

When I was pregnant with the second one there was no problem because Andy was going to nursery school a couple of mornings. And besides, when I was pregnant with Jill, Andy was older [four] so he was capable of going places with me.

My third pregnancy was different in that my second and third children are very close — they're sixteen months apart to the day. We had wanted a third child and I didn't particularly care when he came. I was pleased that I got pregnant when I did with him, just because we were going to be moving again and it was better that he be born before we moved. It was a good time for him to be born, but I probably just was not in the shape physically that I should have been to be having a third. It wasn't that I was sick or anything, I just was feeling awfully tired and really run down, which I didn't feel with the other two.

When I was pregnant with Robert, I had a cleaning lady, and after he was born I had a cleaning lady. Before that I had a kid from college who would come in one day and sit around, and I would go out and do shopping, stuff like that, because Jill was not walking, and it was difficult to get around eight months pregnant carrying this kid who wasn't walking and trying to do anything else.

Although the spacing between Andy and Jill made pregnancy and infant care easier for Alice, she preferred the closer spacing between Jill and Robert. She had wanted a second child earlier.

As a matter of fact, we considered adopting after my older son was born. It was about a four or five year period before I had another child. I had two miscarriages in that period of time and was wondering if I was ever going to have another child. We talked about the fact that if I didn't get pregnant and have a child soon we would adopt. At that time adoptions were possible. Now it would be another story.

All five of Alice's pregnancies were planned. She knew she wanted at least three children and did not want to waste any time since she felt she had started late. She feared the complications associated with increasing maternal age.

The first time I don't remember worrying about abnormalities. I did with my third child — just because I was getting older. I was going to be thirty-four. I tell you, if I were pregnant now, I would probably worry more about that sort of thing.

Her only physical symptom during pregnancy, besides tiredness, was edema, which got worse as each pregnancy progressed.

The day after I was pregnant —it was just ridiculous — I could always tell I was pregnant because my ankles were swollen. I can remember the first time I was pregnant, when I didn't know what was going on, I was not aware of edema, I would wake up in the mornings and my heels would be stiff. I thought, "I'm getting arthritis at an awfully young age." I later found out that my fingers were stiff from edema but for a while I thought it was arthritis. At the end of the pregnancy it would really get unmanageable.

After each baby was born, Alice's mother came to help.

The first one she came and stayed maybe two weeks, maybe even longer, until my father came. The second one my father came up, too, and stayed two to three weeks. The third one she stayed two to three weeks.

Brian was happy to have each child, but became involved as a parent only as the children got older and Alice needed help during and after her third pregnancy.

He would be pleased that we were having another child but never was he going to be involved with the whole thing as far as, "Let's listen to the baby's heartbeat," and that kind of thing. He was not interested; he didn't participate in that way. He was in the labor room with the first child, then when it became apparent that I was not going to have natural childbirth but a Cesarean, he had to leave.

He did not have much to do with caring for any of the infants.

Certainly not with the first one. I mean if I was going to be out and he was going to be home he would give a bottle, the kid wouldn't starve, but if I were around he wouldn't. He doesn't particularly like infants. When the kid begins to have a personality, about eight months, he starts thinking that it might be human. I think you either like babies or you don't like babies.

When I was pregnant with the third one, I was tired a lot, and he would take the other two and play and stuff. They were not infants at this point; the second one was certainly little but she was not an infant. When the youngest was a baby, he would get a bath in the morning. Brian would give the elder two baths at night while I was trying to get the baby settled down. Brian also sort of took over the care of the middle one, getting her up in the morning and getting her dressed and that kind of stuff because the baby would be wanting to eat at that time and the older one had to get off to school. So he was much more of a help then, but he's not really too keen on babies.

Both Alice and Brian share the view that care of the children is her responsibility, with outside help when necessary. In spite of their start as classmates and her employment early in their marriage, they developed a traditional division of labor. Although Alice remembers them as being good friends in the early days, they were always busy with different things and that is even more true now.

I worked and he was in school; we were both very busy. He would usually go back to the library at night because we had a tiny apartment. Then I would usually pick him up, and sometimes we would go out for pizza or something after that and then go home. It was a very college-type of life because that's what the environment was like. We were very close to the people there, the other people in his class.

We were probably closer then than we are now just because there were less things going on in our lives. Now there are more things going on. He is much busier now and pulled off into more different things than then, obviously. I'm not sure that I'm any busier. Well, I have more things to take me out. I suppose I probably expend the same amount of energy as I spent then but it's just running off in different directions.

Their role segregation suits Alice's strong commitment to family, as well as Brian's commitment to his medical career.

In general, it is not the father that stays home with the kids. I think our society does that, not only our society but, obviously, the society of the whole world. It's probably a maternal thing, a thing basic to women as opposed to men. But as far as giving good direction, and being loving and supportive, and being available as a person, I think that applies to fathers as well as mothers.

But my husband is not around as much as lots of other people are —it's just the nature of his profession. Most fathers have dinner with their family every night. Brian does not. He's not around as much as a lot of other fathers are. I think that's just true of all physicians' families.

The fact that Brian returns from work too late to have dinner with the family bothers Alice because she likes the family to be together. But, characteristically, she has adjusted by dealing practically with the reality of her husband's hours. First she tried to hold dinner for him, but that was too difficult for the children. Now she has a set dinner time that meets the children's needs.

The kids and I usually eat at six. If my husband is not here, then he does not. Then it's too bad; we still have dinner because the kids cannot wait any longer. They're starving and start eating a bunch of junk food and then don't eat dinner when we're going to have dinner. Maybe he's home for dinner with us twice a week.

He's usually home on Sunday. He goes in to the hospital on Saturdays and usually takes one or two of the younger kids. They love going to the hospital to see the animals and stuff. It's super fun. He really takes them a lot. He took Jill an awful lot last year. Jill loved going. Now that she is in school every day [kindergarten] she does not go nearly as much, but she likes to go on weekends. He usually takes Robert during the week.

Alice cares for the children and the house.

Somebody's always home, at least now. Jill's home in the morning because she's in kindergarten in the afternoon. Two mornings a week Robert is home, and always in the afternoon. So somebody's always home in the morning, and somebody's always home in the afternoon, unless they're out playing with somebody.

In general, it's straighten up the house, then attack the project for the day. If you're going to the market, or if you're going to go do the laundry, or whatever the project is for the day, handle that. Or there are meetings and stuff that I have to go to, for the school, or for the garden club. There is usually some activity set aside for each day. It depends what I'm doing whether I take the kids. If I'm going to the store, sure. If I'm going to a meeting or something, no, they usually go to a babysitter or they go play with someone.

Alice utilizes a licensed daycare home for occasional daytime sitting. Jill and Robert sometimes go there; Andy is in school full time.

I called the job bank once when I needed a sitter and they gave me a bunch of names. They're all licensed people and I found this woman who's the cheapest person I had used, and I really needed somebody like that. It's worked out very well. It's not that they go there regularly, but if I need a sitter, that's who they go to.

I'm on the Board of Directors of the Garden Club. I'm on the Board of Directors of the PTA, but that's usually done in the evening. That's easy enough; if my husband's not going to be home it's easy to find kids to do babysitting. Daytime sitters are much harder to find.

In addition to their separate activities, Alice and Brian share an active social life.

Across the street there is a tennis/swim club. They have lots of things going on during the winter months, social things. We belong to that and enjoy that a great deal. We bowl in a league there. We have friends for dinner, you know, that kind of socializing. We go to Long Wharf Theater. Sometimes we go to the movies, not a lot but sometimes.

They also have separate recreational activities.

I like to do needlework. He goes to the gym. He plays squash and handball, sometimes he even plays basketball. But that's an irregular thing. It's not like every week he's going to do that. Sometimes he may do it three times a week, and other times he may not want to do it at all.

Most of their socializing is done with friends Alice has made in the neighborhood or Brian has made at the hospital. Although Alice considers two neighborhood women good friends, their best friends, people from medical school, are not nearby. Those school friends are mutual friends from when Alice and Brian were classmates.

I consider my closest friends the people I don't see —the people I really feel close to are the people that I meet once or twice a year. If something catastrophic happens those are the people that I can turn to; they would be the most helpful — like if I needed lots of money or something.

In their twelve years of marriage, Alice and Brian have lived in four different northeastern cities; they have been in their current location for only three years. Their moves have been necessary for Brian's professional advancement. Their first move took them away from his kin and their medical school buddies.

> I didn't mind moving. It's a great way to clean house, let me tell you. If you move every two years, you can't accumulate too much stuff. Just about the time the house is getting pretty grubby, it's time to move on to something nice and clean. I would feel less pleasant about leaving here than I did any other time because, first of all, this is the longest time we've lived in any one house and, secondly, I feel very comfortable in the community. The other places we lived were all very nice but you knew you were there for a short-term period, and so you tended not to get terribly involved in the community. It takes some while to adjust to a new community, and by the time you've gotten yourself settled in you're moving off again. So, I think you tend to hold back from getting yourself involved.

The family lives on Brian's income, which is more than $73,000. Alice manages the finances.

> He just gives me his check and tells me what he thinks he's going to need for the month, and I'll just give him that, and then the rest of the money is mine to do what I want. I end up paying lots of house bills.[2]
>
> I plan this budget every month. It's a totally meaningless thing. I think it's just a matter of sitting down and adding up things and filling out pieces of paper. But as far as being meaningful, no, and I don't understand why. I plan, but then I just never live with it. It is a very paper budget.

Although they live very comfortably, Alice regularly worries about money. As the household billpayer, she is concerned about their high rate of spending, which she does not fully control.[3] Their upcoming summer plans, for example, are causing her tension.

> We are supposed to go to Copenhagen this summer. I just think, "How are we going to be able to afford to go to Copenhagen this summer?" and I get uptight about the whole thing.

He, on the other hand, is sailing around, "We're going to Copenhagen this summer. It's going to be so easy. We're going to buy this car, and we're going to live this way for two months." Meanwhile, we have no one to rent this house, we have not yet found a house there, and I get concerned about it. He does not.

Alice talks to her local friends, not her husband, about her concerns. This further indicates how their relationship has become less close over the years.

I know more about things that bother him than he does about the things that bother me. He talks more; he's more open than I am. I think that's a difference in our personalities. I don't think he has close friends like I do. He has lots of professional friends but he's a very open kind of guy. On the other hand, if he had a real personal problem I guess he would be more likely to keep it to himself until he had it worked out.

Although Brian strongly influences the level of spending, Alice seems to determine the style of family life.

My kids' upbringing probably resembles more the upbringing that I had than what my husband had. His household was much more explosive. His father did lots of hitting and that didn't go on in my house at all. And my household was certainly quieter than his household. But our household is probably looser than mine was. At least my mother thinks so when she comes. She says, "My kids would never do that."

Alice accepts some of her mother's negative judgement and wishes she was more effective at controlling her children.

I wish my kids were a bit more like my brother and I were as kids. My son, the ten-year-old, is somewhat of a problem now. I just didn't act like that at all, I know I didn't. I wouldn't have thought of saying "no" to my mother. I don't know why; I have absolutely no idea why. I was thinking the things that he is saying but I would not say them. If my mother said something I just did it. I didn't say, "I'm not going to do that."

Ultimately Andy does what he is told, but it's always preceded by a scene. I don't mean this is an everyday event, it's just that you can anticipate a battle about something really stupid. I wouldn't have done that with my mother. Not at all.

I can remember my mother making me sit on the chair. I think it was, "You are going to sit in that chair and you can't get out until I come and get you." And the thing that amazes me is that my brother and I would do that. I mean if I told it to my kids now, they would be gone in two minutes. I don't understand why. Why did it work with me but it's not working with them?

Alice greatly admires her mother but sees her own activities as broader.

My mother is a very homebody person who is certainly aware of the world around her and what's going on in it. I think my mother's more of a home person than I will be. Not that I'm running out all the time, but I'm involved in more things now outside of the home than she was on an organizational level. She was very friendly with people in the neighborhood, but I wouldn't say that she was willing to get involved on an organizational level.

In spite of geographical distance, Alice speaks to her parents every week. She keeps in close contact with her brother and members of Brian's extended family as well.

Alice enjoys being a mother, as she perceives her mother did. She does not glorify motherhood, yet she loves having a family.

There are days when I get down. I pick up one room and go back and pick up the same thing I've just done and think, "This can't be what I'm supposed to be spending my time doing." But I think that's a stage they're at.

The ideal mother probably has a lot more patience than I have and yells a lot less. She's probably somebody who is loving and supportive, who will always be there for the kids when they're kids, but who even when they're adult will be there, no matter what kinds of problems they face or they cause. I think that's true of my mother and father.

I asked Alice what she expects to be doing in fifteen years, when her youngest will be twenty.

I have absolutely no idea. I think about maybe going back to the work I did before, but I'm not so sure that that's for me. I wouldn't particularly want to go back to work full time. I just think that's too much of a hassle. Finding a part-time job with any kind of flexibility is really a difficult thing to do, and I think that having to work I would certainly want a flexible enough job. I like the freedom that I have now, that I would not have if I went back to work, and I would very much not want to give it up. I'd like to be able to do the things that I wanted to do — if I wanted to go to an art gallery, I would like to go there.

On the other hand, I could see myself getting more involved in other things. There are all kinds of things going on around town. I could see myself getting involved in community kinds of things. There's been conflict about closing schools, there's concern about sticking a parking lot down where the coop used to be — I could see myself being involved in that kind of stuff, in community affairs.

Motherhood has broadened Alice's interests and activities outside the home.

Having kids is the reason I stay home as opposed to go to work. And because I stay home, I get involved in a lot of things that I really like. I love gardening; I absolutely adore gardening. I could spent hours outside digging. Once I said to my kids, "I'd much rather dig outside in the dirt than be inside in the dirt." I love doing that kind of thing, and I've gotten very interested in horticulture and how to grow things, which I probably wouldn't have gotten involved in if I was not home because of the kids. I've gotten involved in the school PTA-business because I have children. I wouldn't have done that if I hadn't any kids. Because of that I see other things going on in the community that either distress or please me. I certainly have broadened myself, which is certainly a positive thing. I think it's because kids lead you off in different directions.

Alice is a full-time mother and homemaker, as she expected she would be. She acquired a graduate education and positive work experience before she married, which prepared her for planning in important areas of her married life — timing her pregnancies, finding help with childcare when needed, working when financially necessary, coping with her husband's work hours as a doctor, and finding meaningful involvement in community activities. She married a man who shared the strong family values she developed in her close-knit working-class family of origin. While there are some tensions in the marriage about her husband's work hours and spending patterns, their marriage benefits from shared values, her capable management of family matters, and her husband's upper-middle class income. These resources enable Alice to choose and enjoy a family-oriented life and to envision increasing community involvement. She appears content with her choices about motherhood and employment.

3

Elizabeth

I was raised to do everything.

Elizabeth is like Alice in many ways. Both are well educated, middle class, and mobile. Both have stable marriages and three children. Both are also content with their choices about employment. Their choices, however, are different.

While Alice always wanted to be a mother, Elizabeth always wanted a career. She was raised by her widowed father and grew up expecting a full, many-roled life. She married while preparing for her career and established a conjugal relationship based upon a sharing of roles and respect for both partners' career goals. When she became a mother she continued her career commitment and her employment as well. Six of the thirty mothers I interviewed fit this category.

Elizabeth belies the stereotypical image of uncaring, preoccupied, career-oriented mother. She and her husband share strong family values. They spend a great deal of time with their children; their family is their recreation. They organize their work hours to ensure that one of them is with the children most of the time and utilize a regular babysitter three days a week.

Their relationship is mutual, supportive, and sharing. Neither values their career more than their family or their family more than their career; they delight in both of these aspects of their lives. By careful planning and role sharing they are able to reduce the stress and maximize their enjoyment of their multiple roles.

❦ ❦ ❦

I'm definitely sure I didn't want to be a mother when I was a little girl. I thought mothers did a lot of housework or died. I had very negative vibes about mothers per se. I never played with dolls; I had teddy bears who were always sick— probably working out all my fears — they were always bandaged up and in slings and things. I never played with dolls. I was given a doll by my long-suffering grandmother and I took the head off to see how it worked.

Elizabeth was raised by her father; her mother died of cancer when she was three and a half.

We had a housekeeper for eight years and then his widowed sister moved in and was with us from the time I was about eleven until I went to college. But actually, when I was in high school, she became rather ill, and it sort of ended up that we were taking care of her more than she was taking care of us. She left when I was in college; he has lived alone since then.

I think, like any other little girl in those days, I thought weddings were really neat, and swishing around in white dresses and all that was exciting. I also remember thinking that most of the women I knew had pretty dull lives. I didn't have a mother at home, so I didn't have a role model of anyone who was fulfilled doing the domestic business. The lady we had was marvelous, and she was a very affectionate, warm person, but she was also paid for doing it, and I think I knew that when I was very little. I don't ever remember thinking, "Gee, the life of wife and mother is what I want."

I think what I did yearn for was a close relationship. I realized that everybody else had that; after all, in those days nobody had a single parent. I think that when I would go over to other people's houses I rather liked the family idea; I sensed without ever having articulated it that my father didn't have a helpmate, didn't have another person in his life.

Elizabeth always expected to have a career as well as a relationship.

I think I wanted to be a writer as soon as I read *Little Women* I think my father read it to me when I was six or seven. Ironically, I am a writer, although I'm not the kind of writer that I thought I would be when I was seven. I'm still very much into writing and research.

I think I was first allowed to babysit at about thirteen and I did that a lot in high school. I actually made, at the time, quite a bit of money. And then my first real salaried job was when I was seventeen; it was between my junior and senior years in high school. I worked in the catering department of a very large bakery and catering company. It was very much like working in a factory, and it was fun because I was earning minimum wage, which at the time was eighty cents an hour! But it was also terribly boring work — I would do things like butter bread for eight hours, and I went nuts. I think that was one of the things that made me determined that I was going to get a profession: I had to do something to prevent this from becoming my career.

Her father expected a great deal from her, and she internalized these expectations.

When I was a girl, I was raised to do everything. I was raised to play the piano, to do well in school, to be a good athlete, to be a lady, to wear white gloves. I used to jokingly say that my father raised me to be a member of the junior league, a wife, a mother, and then if I wanted to be an academic, too, that was just fine. It never occurred to him that these things had to be choices. I think I spent high school and maybe part of my college and early professional years trying to do all things — making all the bread, being the perfect domestic one, in addition to being the best graduate student and all that. Pretty soon it dawned on me that you couldn't do all these things, that you had to make choices or else your health was going to crumble.

Elizabeth grew up in the midwest in a family of two. Her father was a manufacturer's agent who, although middle class, was always subject to the tensions of an uncertain income. He was also a very giving parent.

He is an extremely affectionate person, and he is one who has spent an awful lot of time with me. Sunday afternoons we always did something: we went to a museum, we went to concerts, we went for a walk around the park, or went hiking in the country if it was nice weather. I don't remember very many Sundays that we didn't do something. Saturdays we did a lot of errands — we did the grocery shopping and riding around after. He always got home early enough so that he was around; we ate dinner together. From the time when I was very small, he always ate dinner with me if he was home.

He did the shopping and lots of picking up stuff, but the housekeeper did the basic domestic work. He was a great breakfast cook because he had been a bachelor for a long time; he could make eggs and bacon and things like that. When the housekeeper left and my Aunt Miriam came and would occasionally get sick, he and I would sort of learn to cook together, beyond his earlier capabilities, because we got sick of eating the same foods all the time. I remember going to the bookstore and buying *Joy of Cooking* when I was eleven or twelve. We wanted gravy. We had a roast and we wanted to learn how to make gravy.

But he was not a demonstratively emotional person. I don't remember his saying things like "I love you" — it would have embarrassed him. He certainly showed it, and I certainly knew it. He read to me every night before I went to bed, gave lots of hugs and things like that, but I don't remember him saying in so many words, "I love you." It's something that I try to do with my own children because he didn't do it for me. I just feel it's too bad not to be able to verbalize it.

Elizabeth attended a private girls' school from seventh grade through high school, then went east to attend Smith College.

I had some notion that my mother had wanted to go to Smith, and, therefore, "I'm going to Smith for my mother." I don't know if that's really true. My father, of course, always dated Smithies, all the way through Dartmouth. I think I just had this feeling: "Carry on the family position." I think my father would have been very disappointed if I had said I wanted to stay home and go to school nearby. I think he very much wanted me to go away; I think he wanted me to go to Smith, as a matter of fact.

She spent her junior year abroad at a Canadian university and the summer between her junior and senior years in Europe. She met Walter while touring Europe. They spent a casual afternoon together and did not even exchange last names. In the fall he looked her up at Smith and they started dating.

> We went out together that year, my senior year, and I think that spring I was pretty serious about this guy. I was also very serious about my career. I remember our deciding very coldly and rationally that we didn't want to take on the first year of graduate school and the first year of marriage at the same time. And so we didn't; we got married a year after that.

Before starting to date each had applied to graduate school at Berkeley.

> We both got in. God knows what would have happened if we hadn't, but we did. We went there unmarried, sort of unofficially engaged. We got officially engaged in November. We got married the next summer. My father was determined to roll out the wedding of the century, and he couldn't do it by himself, so I had to go back and do the mother-of-the-bride bit for myself and get myself married. He would never have been able to pull it off.

During the early years of their marriage, Elizabeth and Walter did their doctoral work and launched their careers.

> Our relationship was very good; it was very academic. I think we had a lot of mutual interests, although we were not in the same field. No problems — just had a good time. We worked very hard; we didn't go out a lot and do a lot of socializing.

At the time of the interviews, Elizabeth was thirty-eight, Walter was forty, and their three children were eight, five, and two. Elizabeth was a college professor, Walter a research associate at a different university. They owned the comfortable home in which they lived.

They carefully planned the timing of their first child, who was born six years after they married.

We simply sat down and figured it out. He is a biologist after all and he knew the biological reasons for having children reasonably early. At that point we both had teaching experience, we had this house already, so we were settled. We were financially at the point where it would not be a drain to have a babysitter. We felt that I probably could finish my dissertation if I stopped teaching and had the child. I probably couldn't do the three things, but I could do the two. So it was really a calculation based on several variables.

When we were first married, we really didn't talk about having children. I think we just thought, "Someday we will probably have babies, but this is very much in the future." When we got to the point of five or so years of marriage, we simply thought, "It's about time; we don't want to be too much older; we don't want to wait too much longer." We had this myth that it would probably take us six or eight months, so we might as well start. It turned out that it didn't, but that's doctors' advice — don't race right in and assume you are going to get pregnant the next minute.

So it was a very calculated decision. In fact, one of my husband's running jokes, every time he sees one of these movies where women come fluttering in and throw their arms around their husbands and say, "Guess what, dear!" is, "You never did that. You always asked me two months ahead of time! Why don't we do these romantic things — roses, knitting booties!" It was not that way.

Elizabeth had few expectations and little support for her first pregnancy.

I wasn't around very many people having babies; my friends were all academics. I don't ever remember having a close pregnant friend. Those who were from college were always five thousand miles away and I sent them a silver spoon and that was it. I don't remember being afraid. I don't remember thinking anything much about it, except that this was a perfectly normal process and that I would probably do it — it wasn't a very great concern.

I remember the first visit to the obstetrician he started asking me things like, "Do you want to breastfeed?" And I had never thought about it, but said, "Well, sure, why not! This is the way one does it, or we wouldn't be here after ten thousand evolutions, so I think so." But I had never really read books, I never had sat down and planned these things out. I remember having seen a film in college, one of those awful old-fashioned childbirth films where they put a black band across the mother's eyes and then show you the obstetrician's eye view, and I remember thinking, "This is really sickening, and I don't want to watch, and I don't want to be very much involved in it." But I don't remember being afraid; I just remember thinking it was kind of yucky.

I did not want to use anesthetic because I had ether when I was eleven and it made me really sick, and it scared me to death. I think to any intellectual person, probably the thought of being put to sleep, you are afraid you are never going to wake up. Your identity is your mind; if somebody is going to put me to sleep, I'm just going to become a vegetable. So my feeling was, "I will go through anything other than be put to sleep."

Like many women committed to continuing their careers while embarking on motherhood, Elizabeth was glad to be expecting a child but not overjoyed with the experience of pregnancy. She had no models for being a pregnant college professor.

My first pregnancy was not uncomfortable — I taught right up until the end. I did not particularly enjoy being pregnant. I didn't hate it, but I wasn't the type to sit around contemplating my growing navel. I guess I found it in a faint way embarrassing because at that point nobody in academic life ever did this. I think it was a little uncomfortable to stand up and do things like give papers at meetings, or lecture to people, or teach, and colleagues tended not to mention it, even when I was practically ready to pop. I think I felt it was a little awkward. Maybe that's not true so much anymore.

I thought, "Okay, this is the way you get babies, I want babies." I didn't sit around glowing. I don't mean I hated it, but I think I was fairly neutral about it. I looked forward to having it over with. I didn't like the way I looked. I don't think it bothered me particularly, but I didn't go around jumping into maternity clothes in the sixth week, looking forward to saying "I'm pregnant." There wasn't anything I particularly liked about it. I disliked being fat, being ungainly, having trouble moving around a little bit. I'm not very comfortable that way. It's sort of like being five pounds overweight and wishing that you weren't.

I remember at one point, toward the end of the first pregnancy, thinking, "My goodness, I'll never be alone again," and being worried about that because I'd always enjoyed being alone a lot. I didn't like feeling that somehow I had been invaded and that I might never be really alone again. I think that was not true, in retrospect. I've been alone a lot; I don't think it changed very much, but I remember an afternoon's worth of subtly having this occur to me and thinking, "I wonder if I'm going to miss this."

Walter's involvement with the pregnancy was also down-to-earth.

I think he was very helpful, very matter-of-fact; he was interested but he didn't go wild. He read books, he went to Lamaze classes with me, but he wasn't romantically intrigued. I used to say, "Don't you want to feel a foot?" And he would say, "Yuck, no, not especially." On the other hand, he was very supportive. I think he was good for me because he didn't encourage me to wallow in it either, but if I felt like talking about it he didn't turn me off.

Her first pregnancy was very easy.

I think I had a couple of weeks of nausea with the first but not very much. That was much worse with my later pregnancies, as a matter of fact. I was just very lucky — I didn't have any backaches; I didn't have all the usual things that people complain about. Other than not feeling very good for a couple of weeks somewhere around the thirteenth or fourteenth week, I don't remember any discomfort. The first pregnancy was the most comfortable. I got increasingly nauseated, more so in the second one and more so in the third. I also, as everybody does I suppose, gained more weight with each one and had bigger babies with each one. And I was also that much older with each one, so who knows.

Elizabeth's low key attitude about her pregnancies did not carry over into the deliveries. She was well prepared, having taken Lamaze classes with Walter. All three deliveries were by natural childbirth.

I think, as every woman is, I was unsure. One never knows exactly what it is going to feel like, no matter how many films you watch or how much you read. I don't remember anything that I would really call fear. It was more apprehension and uncertainty. I was afraid of anesthetics, and still am, and I was determined that I wasn't going to take any — not because I wanted to be courageous but I think for two reasons: One, because I was really afraid of losing my mind, quite literally, and secondly because I've always been somebody who likes experiences, and I wanted to know what all this was about. I remember a friend who had a baby saying to me, "Oh, it was so comfortable, they put me to sleep and then I woke up and they told me I had a boy." I remember being really turned off and thinking, "My goodness, it's like having your appendix out, I don't want that. I want to be there. I want to know what it's like. I want to know that the baby's all right the minute that it's born. I want to know what it is. I don't want to be out of it."

The births were all very nice. In fact, I remember saying after the first one that delivery for me was really sort of redemption. I hadn't enjoyed the pregnancy much, had kind of tolerated it, but I really liked delivering babies. It was a lovely experience.

Elizabeth had no outside help after Rosa, her first child, was born, so she prolonged her hospital stay by a day. She came home four days after giving birth. Her hospital stay was only two days with each of the other children.

After the second, my mother-in-law came for a little before and a week afterwards. And then my father came when Jesse was born. He and Walter divided everything right down the pipe. My father did the cooking and the dishes, and Walter did the kids and the laundry. He stayed for a week, and he loved it. He had a baby when fathers were kept away for about six weeks because they were germy and incompetent. He loved it. He came in to see Jesse the next morning, and Jesse was named after him and my father-in-law, so he was really thrilled with the whole thing. I don't think he'd seen such a tiny baby, certainly not to be able to hold it. He was marvelous and intrigued with the whole thing. I think he heartily enjoyed it.

I remember being a bit more on sort of an emotional teeter-totter after the babies were born. I would either get the giggles, or, if something happened that was sad, it would sort of wipe me out. If academic pressure intensified, it would be that much more intense than it was normally. I had nothing like postpartum depression, just swings of emotion that I felt were hormonally caused. I could almost feel myself revving up when it was time to nurse the baby.

Elizabeth nursed all three of her children, for eight and one half, thirteen, and sixteen months respectively.

I enjoyed breastfeeding. I thought that it was a lovely way to have sort of enforced leisure, especially with the second and third one when there was another one around wanting to be read to and all. It's a nice way of being sure that you have time for the newborn, and I thought that was good. I also just had a very strong sort of biological feeling about it, that this was a good system, that nature had intended it this way. The race had obviously evolved this way, and, if you could do it, it was very healthy. And I liked it. I thought it was easy. With Jesse [the youngest] if I had had to get up in the night and warm a bottle, it would have done me in. It was all I could do to get up.

I think, if anything, having a child made our marriage better. I don't think it did anything very radical to it, but what was really nice was seeing each other in a new role, that somebody you care about and someone you had a very good relationship with as a friend, as an intellectual companion, is suddenly someone you see as a father. It was nice. He has always been a very involved father, a very participating father, loves his children, likes to play with them, likes to be with them. I think that was obvious from the first five minutes, and it was just nice to see someone you care about in that new role. I don't remember ever feeling that it created tensions and all the things you read about. That just didn't happen.

Walter and Elizabeth were committed to both of their careers. As two professional people they planned to share family responsibilities and have outside help.

I think we just assumed that we would hire a babysitter and that we would share a lot of the childcare. I don't remember feeling conflicted. I think initially we thought we would get someone who would come here, and then it just happened that the lady we got said she couldn't come here, but she could take the baby at her house, and that turned out to be an advantage because then we could work at home.

Starting from eight or nine weeks, I did the same three-days-a-week thing. I have the babysitter three days a week,Monday, Wednesday, Friday, and then also work during naptimes the other days, and in the evenings. I have had the same babysitter for nine years, which must be some kind of modern miracle. She's two and a half blocks away; she is an Irish mother, fantastic, dedicated to the needs and interests of children. She had her own children very, very young. She is not a great deal older than I am, but when we first started with her, her youngest child was nine. She wanted to be home when the child came home for lunch, but she also needed some money. She has always taken our infants at her house. We are an embarrassingly planned family, all exactly three years apart, so she had each child for three years and then, when they went to nursery school, she picked up with the next one.

Elizabeth was able to control the timing of her children exactly. Since her teaching commitments ran from September through May, she timed her babies for early June. This enabled her to be home the first eight or nine weeks without missing classes.

The first time we thought maybe in the next six months sometime we might want to have a baby, and it turned out that the minute we tried we did. After that we thought maybe we could do it that way the second and third time, and, as it happened, that was the case. So, by then we were sort of joking about it, saying why don't we have one on June 5th. Their birthdays are three years apart almost to the day.

When her family was complete she continued to control her fertility by electing sterilization.

I had my tubes tied two years after Jesse was born. We both decided that we didn't want to do it right after Jesse, partly for practical reasons, since we understood it would be an added stay in the hospital, but also we both felt we didn't want to do it in the kind of postpartum feeling. We wanted to be really sure that we intended to do this. I talked it over with my doctor and he said it was better to wait until you really felt that you had handled all the awful contingencies that can happen and you're that much farther from having a newborn infant.

This careful planning was a consistent trait of Elizabeth and Walter's.

They already shared responsibility for household tasks before Rosa was born.

Years and years ago, before we ever had kids, we sat down and really talked about the whole housework business in a real time and motion way — my husband had his engineering degree. And we decided that we would be very careful about things that had something to do with health or things that really bothered people: that if somebody had a real thing about a straight living room we would do the straight living room, but we would not do things that didn't pose a health risk and didn't bother us. We just decided that unmade beds did not bother either one of us and that we were not going to become slaves to the notion that you had to have a made bed to be a decent person. Basically nobody makes the beds, but the cleaning lady changes them once a week. Laundry we split. I do the clothes; Walt does the sheets and towels. He does the buttons;

I do the sewing with a needle and thread. He does the buttons with one of those buttonnaire things.

In addition to household tasks, they also share financial responsibilities. Their joint earnings are between $55,000 and $64,000 a year, depending upon variability in book royalties. They live modestly, except for their children's private school tuitions. They rotate the task of paying the bills.

We are both natively very frugal. If there is any sort of unusually large expense we work it in, but we try not to do two of those kinds of things in a year. But I wouldn't say we budget in the same sense as friends of mine do, where they actually sit down and allocate every penny. We really lucked out on housing. We got this house when the housing prices were tolerable. We got very good rates for it, and we really don't have very heavy housing expenses, which is just a blessing.

Generally Walt pays the bills this year because he's home more. He kind of writes the checks as they come in. Neither of us can stand the idea of taking an evening out and doing it for the month, so we usually try to keep up with it as they come in. We always pay our own professional bills, things like fees for journal subscriptions, or the cap and gown I just had to rent. That kind of thing we do individually. Joint expenses for running the house and so on usually this year he does because he's home when the bills come in, and he can just sit down and write the check and send it off quickly.

This cooperative sharing of roles, in conjunction with careful scheduling, enables Elizabeth to continue to work full time after having children, with relatively little stress. She and her husband are equally responsible for picking up the children after school and babysitter and taking them to their various after-school activities.

Our attempt is to be quite fair with each other and to do it something like two days each, and then the fifth day we see who has got the biggest burden. It depends really upon whose needs are the greatest. We have been lucky this year that very seldom has anybody really had to give up something that really matters. And if it did, it was who announced first. Last Thursday we all had, ironically even the children all had, something we wanted to do. I had put in a claim about a month before that there was a seminar that I particularly wanted to attend and a person I had been invited to meet, so I just did it. My husband could have, I suppose, gotten an afternoon babysitter and gone to his, but it turned out that he decided that it was easier not to.

Elizabeth feels that her ability to work has improved by having children.

I think it organized us, at least me. My husband has always been pretty well-organized. Believe it or not, I think it made me a better thinker because I think it disciplined me. I realized, okay, you've got until three o'clock, or whatever, and you've got to get this amount done and thought through. I think before I tended to go up every possible little alleyway. I couldn't write a word until I read the last eighty-five things written on it. And I think I cut that out, I think I became a more efficient worker; I used my time better; I didn't fritter it away.

I also think there is something very joyous in the contrast between a child and academic work because academic work is selfish and narrowly focused. You can't be interrupted; it's not sociable. A child is just the opposite. A child is selfless, and broadly focused, and demanding, also very sociable, and you can play with them. When I got really sick of the dissertation, I had the baby. When I got sick of the baby, I had the dissertation. It was really a very nice balance.[1]

My husband has never been a nine-to-five person; I think that's why he likes academic work. He likes flexibility, and he is a very quick worker. He has always done a lot of things; he has always had a lot of hobbies and a lot of projects. We laugh that there was one scene that a friend of mine noticed; I didn't because he is like this all the time. She came in and the TV was on, my mother-in-law was visiting, and my husband was sitting at his desk holding the baby in one arm and sort of jostling her on his shoulder while writing an academic paper. Jeanne came in and said, "What are you doing?" and he said,

"I'm writing such and such an article." And she said, "This is absurd! No one can work like this." But he can, he truly can. He can talk to his mother, hold the baby, have the TV going, and still think. Now, admittedly, he wasn't solving a differential equation, but he was doing something useful. He's like that — he's remarkable. I cannot do that, but he really can, so I honestly don't think having a child set him back.

I think he did feel that he wasn't the typical Yale assistant professor who worked ninety hours a week and went to the lab every night. I don't think he would have been without children and having children he's less inclined to do that. He's a family man. He was also an only child, and it's nice not to have only children. I think we like our family; we just like our family life.

Elizabeth puts neither career nor family first.

People who are basically housewives and mothers have often said, "What are your priorities? Now, don't you really put your children first, and don't you really feel that you put your professional life second and you really live for your children?" On the other hand, women who are basically career women have often said to me, "Don't you really find the children are just sort of an obstacle and your main goal is the career?" I keep resisting saying yes to either one of them because I really think that, aside from things like if a child becomes ill, I don't think there are fixed priorities. I think that the priorities shift from month to month and day to day. I remember when Aaron was going into first grade, right round the time that Jesse was born, he seemed to go through a period of being very nervous; he didn't want me out of his sight. He needed a lot of attention that particular summer that his sister didn't need and even a newborn baby didn't need. The baby could be lying on my lap and get all of his mothering while Aaron was getting a lot of personal attention. On the other hand, right now I've got that lovely stack of term papers to do. I will probably not take time to do something with a child that I would do three weeks from now when the semester is over. I think it's very important for anyone who takes on this multiple-roles business to realize that priorities shift. It's truly not that your career is more important, or really your children are.

They're all very important, and they keep getting rearranged almost on a daily, certainly on a weekly basis.

Taking care of their two jobs, their three children, and their dog leaves Elizabeth and Walter very little free time.

What do you do with your spare time? The answer is, "What is that?" I would say basically an awful lot of things with the family. We usually try to do an outing at least every weekend. We cut out of the newspaper interesting things to do and have a file that we put them into, like maple syruping, apple picking, county fairs, zoos, things like that. We usually try to do one outing a weekend, sometimes more, but it depends on the season. We often do things with another family who have kids roughly the same age as ours. Sometimes it means them coming over for lunch and letting the kids play and having some adult conversation.

Neither of us plays any kind of sport regularly. We used to play tennis but we don't like to pay for babysitting to do it. I haven't been to a movie since Aaron was born, I don't think. Walt loves movies and he goes to movies a lot. I'm just not a media person. Sometimes he goes to matinees in the daytime, if he has time off, because I don't like to go. He used to have a great crony whose wife hated the movies too and the two of them went all the time but, sadly enough, they moved away.

We have a season subscription to Long Wharf Theater. We take advantage of a lot of free things at the university that come along. We occasionally go out to dinner with friends, though it's been a lot less often the last few years. It must be something about our lives suddenly that we're just so busy that the motivation for organizing a dinner party is not really there very often. As a matter of fact, I think I've had about five dinner parties this January, and they've all been on the spur of the moment, "We've got a refrigerator full of spaghetti sauce, come on over." They were lovely. I like them like that because you don't have to fuss for two days ahead of time. But I do like to entertain. I enjoy dinner parties. I love to cook and I would do it more often if I didn't mind spending the two days.

We get a babysitter and go out about once a month. As a matter of fact, we have never joined a babysitting pool because

we don't go out often enough, and we've always been concerned about getting really boxed-in and losing evening work
hours. In fact, we do it so seldom that our kids really complain
when we do it; we keep telling them a lot of people go out twice
a week, but they just aren't used to it.

I think we spend more time together than other people I
know, and I value that. I sense that a lot of people that I know
kind of want to get away from their children. They feel burdened. They are always looking for times to plan something
when they don't have to be involved with the children. I don't
feel that. I think we probably enjoy each other more than some
married couples I know who seem to like to do a lot of things
with other people, and sometimes you wonder if they are
avoiding doing things together because they don't like to. In
other words, I think we may value the old traditional notion
of family life more than other people seem to. I think we have
a tremendous sense of responsibility to one another and to the
kids, and I think it's very mutual, which is what makes it work.

I feel very responsible for my husband's own satisfactions
and happiness and professional fulfillment, and I think he
does for me. When one of us has some kind of triumph— we
publish a paper, or win an award, or get a book out—we
celebrate as if it belonged to both of us, and we articulate this
to each other. It's almost as if it's the same career and I'm just
as thrilled when he gets something as I am when I get something, and I think vice versa. It's very mutual.

Elizabeth is very satisfied with her marriage, her family, her
career. I asked her to project fifteen years into the future, when
her youngest would be seventeen.

I don't expect to be doing anything all that radically different. I hope I'll have published some more books. I hope I still
like the work I'm doing. I don't expect radical transformations.
I'm ambitious academically — I hope people will have heard
of me — I hope I have a lot of bibliography behind me. But as
far as any major qualitative change, no. I hope I'm still married, but a little less harried. We won't have anyone who cries
in bed anymore, I hope. At least Jesse now announces that he's
"frying" in bed. He doesn't just cry, which is one advance, and

it's "frying" because he can't say "C." So he says, "Mommy, come get me, I'm frying." Generally it's a nightmare.

She is extremely positive about the effect on her life of having children.

I would say it has been altogether positive. I think it's enriched my marriage because I've seen my husband in a new role, or a series of new roles, as a parent. On the practical level, it's made me more organized. I don't procrastinate as much as I used to. I have finally gotten the family which I did not have growing up, and I really like it.

I feel that I live very much in the present, and I don't plan ahead as much as I used to. I think I spent most of my twenties kind of "when I get my dissertation finished," "when I get the book out," "when I get this article written." In fact, I remember one time when we were in graduate school we had some kind of set-to and I accused my husband of really being unpleasant and he said, not altogether as a joke, "Oh, I'll be nice when I get my dissertation written." I think it was a joke; on the other hand, he was perfectly serious that there was going to come this utopian time when we wouldn't have pressures on us and everything would be very easy.

I think that we have realized that that time is never going to come. We're always going to be very pressured, we're always going to be busy, there are always going to be eighty-five more things to do than there is time in which to do them. And so I think we've learned not to say "someday we have to do that." I think that's what maturity means: coming to grips with the present and not always projecting into the future.

Yet, there are professional costs to her choices.

I went to a conference about four years ago and the topic that we discussed was "Can a feminist scholar who has multiple roles perform at the highest professional level?" That was a real toughy because then, four years ago, I kept insisting yes, damn it, I'm just as smart as anybody else. I think now I might modify that. If you're talking about becoming *the expert* in a field and putting out the sixty-hour weeks that you would have to do to achieve that, the answer is probably no. But I also think that's not a question for women, it's a question for people. I think the same thing is true for men. You read about people who are in high levels of government service who never see their families. I think that's a choice that people have to make: what kind of people they want to be. When I do commit myself to writing a book, writing a paper, doing a study, I try to do it at the highest professional level. I make sure that that task is the best I can make of it. But as far as saying I have to get ten books out by the time I'm forty-five, no.

Elizabeth's approach to life is a wonderful example of good planning. She has the career she always wanted to have; she also has a fine family. She carefully thought about and planned when to marry, when to have children, when to have a tubal ligation. She plans childcare arrangements, daily schedules, and housekeeping. Importantly, she does not do this alone. She and Walter have a relationship built upon mutual respect, egalitarian principles, and strong family values. Her middle-class background, her strong relationship with her father, and her high level of academic and professional achievement all contribute to her choices, and her choices clearly contribute to her happiness. She fully enjoys her combination of career and motherhood.

4

Linda

Family life is the only happiness.

Linda, like Alice, grew up in a working-class environment where she developed a strong desire to have a family. Unlike Alice, however, she has only a high school education and has never left the locality in which she was raised. Although the idea of teaching interested her as a high school student, she did not think of it as a realistic goal; she expected to be a wife and mother, not to have a career. After high school she got a job so she could buy herself the clothes and things her family could not afford.

She met and married a local man, and within a few months gave up her job to make a home. Soon after, she discovered she was pregnant. Since marriage and motherhood were her goals, she felt "free and easy" about having children; none of her five pregnancies were planned. Her upper-middle-class marriage is a big step up the socio-economic ladder; she is proud of her home and her family.

Linda's views about family life are quite traditional. Her husband helps with the five children when he is around, but he has a very busy work schedule. She accepts her roles as homemaker, wife, and mother with devotion, and passes judgment on other mothers who do not. She does little planning for the future and tries to accept things as they come along. Although she shows some signs of stress, she also expresses many satisfactions.

❦ ❦ ❦

When I was a little girl, I wanted to be exactly what I am now — married, happy, with children — the whole typical role of motherhood, having babies. I think I always saw it more in terms of babies in my arms, feeding babies, playing with my children, picnics, things like that.

Linda was the youngest in a working-class family with four children, two girls and two boys. Neither parent completed high school; her father left school at the age of nine to help earn money for his family. Both of her parents worked in factories, although her mother stayed home with Linda until she was in school.

While Linda was growing up, social life revolved around the extended family, and her mother was the center of that family.

When I think of what we had as a family — there was always, I kid you not, always someone at my dinner table. People would come in and eat, all relatives always came to our house because it was — my mother was — the center of the family. She was not the oldest, but she just had a way. She'd always get a meal on. She was really a hot ticket. She'd always have a joke, a dirty joke, not gross but these cute little jokes. She was a roar as far as the life of the party goes. She'd always have you laughing all the time; she was loving, very affectionate — which I am too, and it's from her. Always hugging, kissing; I mean when I was twenty, I'd think nothing of going and sitting on her lap. She'd get silly and stuff like that.

She was a really nice person, but she was domineering. She loved us all around her. She was a big family person. See, I'm like that. She liked everybody around her hearth. She was very outspoken. I can remember when I was becoming aware of social status, when I started to get out in the world and meet people who were better than us on a social standing, I would get a little annoyed with my mother because she would be a little loud — so out with everything that she would embarrass me sometimes. That was maybe in my early twenties.

She was the center. There was definitely that in our house, the matriarchal complex, or whatever you want to call it. She was the center of the house; everything centered around my mother. My father loved it because it brought everything to him. He had the shyer, more reserved personality. She did dominate him, not to the point where he was a sniveling little person, but she did control. Like she'd say, "We're going out to dinner tonight," or, "We're having a Christmas party." She handled all the finances. She took care of everything; you see, my father was not educated. I mean he could read, but I would not say he would be able to sit down and write if you dictated something to him. He would probably have trouble with that. She had more education, so she controlled that part of it, too. She handled all the money and things like that.

Linda's family was poor. They always had adequate food and clothing, but Linda missed having the variety of clothes and things that other kids had.

I worried about boys, being accepted. I can remember not having the right clothes, not being dressed quite right. I had a lot of friends that had a lot more than I did. They accepted me and I always looked okay, but I never quite had the outfit that was "the outfit." There was the pleated skirt and the white sweater and I never quite did that. That's probably why I went to work and was able to start to get things of my own. That meant something to me at that age.

Also, I did have a physical problem: my teeth were bad. I had a big space between my teeth, and that was one of my biggest problems in life. I felt very self-conscious. There was never a picture of me with my mouth open. I always smiled with my lips tight and close. I used to think that it didn't bother me, but it did. I had it corrected when I could afford it. I had it done when I was about twenty-one years old. As a teenager and as a young adult, I had plenty of boyfriends, and I had plenty of dates and the whole bit. I was never pushed aside because I think I had a nice personality, but inside it bothered me. It was always a source of embarrassment for me, and they could never afford to have my teeth done. So when I finally got that last job where I was making good money, I bought a car, and I went and had my teeth fixed.

Linda started working part-time as a file clerk when she was sixteen. By the time she graduated from high school, she had worked her way up to receptionist and continued the job full time. She wanted to earn money and did not really consider college as an option.

> My parents were not the type to push me towards education; that was not a big thing. I had a lot of friends who went on to college and stuff like that, but I wasn't going in that direction. The other thing was financial. I did not have good enough marks to get a scholarship, and my parents did in no way have the funds to put me through school. And I didn't know enough — were there loans? — I don't even remember. Did my counselor tell me that I could pay for it later, or work part time and go to school? I didn't know those things then. It just didn't seem like an option to me.

Although Linda was attracted to teaching, she did not pursue it. Having a career was not important to her; having a family was.

> I always felt teaching would be a very rewarding occupation. I loved children. I have this personality; I am a great helper. I love kids; I get a lot of enjoyment working with children. I've done it now; I'm getting it through the church and my own family.

Instead, Linda worked and dated while she continued to live at home.

> The love that was generated in my family of growing up, I wanted that feeling for myself. I wanted children, too: that was the role I accepted in life. I felt, if anything, maybe a pressure to get married. I can't say I got married because of pressure but that was the most important, that took precedence over a career — marriage and family. A career was not number one in my mind, not as it is for some women today. I think more women have that feeling, but to me family life is the only happiness. I know nothing else. So I wanted that for myself.

Marriage was what Linda was after, but her courtship disappointed any girlhood dreams of romance.

> I met Jerry at a friend's house when I was twenty-two. I had a girlfriend who was my age and she had a brother Jerry's age. I'm a year and a half older than Jerry, something like that. We used to go over to the house and met through mutual friends. Jerry was shy. Jerry was on the reserved side, and I was crazy about him, but he didn't have the nerve to ask me out. So we all went to a movie one night as a group; then from there it became dating. I dated him for two years, and I went in and out of love a couple of times and then finally decided that this was it and that was that. We got engaged and got married six months later.

Her decision to marry was a practical one: Jerry was a good catch.

> Jerry loved me. When I met Jerry, he was really ivy league, and I was just getting on my feet as far as my own self. I thought that he was neat, and then when I finally got to know him, he wasn't as cool as I thought he was. So I was crazy about him when I met him, and then after I started dating him I thought this guy isn't so terrific. So I fell madly in love and then out of love, and then we had many dates and I liked him, and he was a little bit of a let down in the middle. Then I finally, after all this surface emotional thing came out, I realized that he was terrific — he was a good catch. So, we dated heavily. He always wanted to marry me; I was the one who was more evasive. I had a lot of dates, I was going here and there, I was loose and fancy-free. But then I decided that he was it, that he would be the man for me. When we were married (I always say this to him anyway), he loved me more than I loved him. I'm not saying I didn't love him; I loved him, but I love him a hundred times more now than I did then. Our relationship has blossomed and keeps blossoming into something more beautiful.

Linda and Jerry had a big church wedding with a buffet dinner.

I lived in the lowest section of Westville, and they lived up
near the Yale Bowl which is the other side of the tracks, so to
speak. His father was in the city government at that time, and
then lots of important people had to be invited to the wedding.
All this kind of stuff, which was really big stuff for my family.
They were really impressed with all this. And his family paid
for some of the wedding, and my mother just managed to get
the money together, and I helped out. I bought my own gown
and flowers.

Linda and Jerry went to Bermuda for their honeymoon but
returned a day or two later when Linda's sixty-year-old mother
died of a heart attack.

The first six months of my marriage were overshadowed by
my mother's death. I can't say I was depressed or miserable,
but it was a factor in our marriage. And my father was the type
that was so dependent on her that he was a concern of ours.
But Jerry being the type of guy he was, it worked out. We did
not have marital problems or anything like that. And then I
became pregnant, and, of course, everything centered around
me and the pregnancy.

At the time of the interviews, Linda was thirty-seven, Jerry
was thirty-five, and their five children were ten and a half, nine,
seven, five, and five months. Linda was a homemaker, Jerry
owned a real estate company. They owned the large, attractive
home in which they lived, as well as a beach home in which they
spent their summers.

Linda and Jerry did not even discuss using contraception
when they were first married. He was Catholic, and she wanted
six children.

We were just free and easy. If I got pregnant, I got pregnant.
I have used birth control since then, but from the day I got
married, for many years, we used nothing. I wanted children:
that was the role I accepted in life. I was twenty-five when I
got married. I certainly had the option to go on to a career, and
go to college and do anything I wanted, or to be married. I got
married because that was the most important.

Linda had been working full time for seven years when she married. She had changed jobs twice and was making good money. She stopped working six months after her wedding. Jerry was doing well in real estate. He had joined a family company when he left college and was already established when they married.

I was pregnant when I quit, but I didn't know it. I was like a week pregnant, and then, after I quit, I found out I was pregnant. Isn't that something! I quit on the twelfth and I conceived on the sixth — it was one of those kinds of things. I don't know why I quit. I guess just to be home and to start a family — that was what it was. We were married in June, I quit in December, and I was going to relax and kind of have the spring to get my apartment organized and everything, and then I figured we could have our family in the summertime.

Linda loved being pregnant.

There's nothing like the first pregnancy. There's no question about that; it's really beautiful. It was fine. I had no ill effects. I thought I was beautiful. I felt beautiful. I loved the attention. I loved the life movement. It was wonderful for me — that's why I've had so many. But, I don't care what any mother says, there is nothing like the first. I love all my children, but Missy, it's not that I would take her over Jordan or Brian or Kimmy, but there are things that I did with Missy — she was my teacher. She was my teacher.

Subsequent pregnancies were also physically easy for Linda, but a couple were associated with emotional pressure.

I had no difficulties. But when I was having Kimmy, which was my fourth, I was concerned that she would be abnormal simply because I had three beautiful children, and I thought, "How is it possible that the Lord could be so good to me that I would have another one," and I was concerned. My second pregnancy my father was ill, and I went through that period with him. He had cancer when I was pregnant with Jordan, and I was very emotionally upset during that time, and I was concerned about her simply because I was so emotional and distraught that I thought I was going to maybe do something to the baby.

I had no difficulties with my pregnancies, but I was very conscious of my figure. If any time in my life I looked the most well-groomed, it was when I was pregnant, because I felt as if I had to make up for this. I pride myself on my figure, and I didn't like the fact that I was big, especially afterwards. Maybe not so much during, but those first few months afterwards you're like awful, and I hate that. See, I don't like fat. So I didn't like the weight gain. I can eat anything and not gain weight, except when I'm pregnant. I didn't like gaining weight. And the highs and lows of the moods. Less control over your own emotional state; it's harder to exert control.

Although Linda loved being pregnant and happily anticipated having an infant, her enthusiasm did not encompass childbirth. Fifteen of the twenty-nine women I interviewed prepared for their first delivery by attending Lamaze or hospital-run classes and by reading as much as they could.[1] Of the other fourteen, six talked to other women about childbirth and did some reading, while Linda and seven others were so fearful that they made a point of not even thinking about it.[2]

Emotionally I felt that it was all going to be gooshy- gooshy. You're laying there in a pink nightgown, and the baby's nursing, and it's all beautiful and wonderful. I had no idea about the hospital part, and I didn't want to know. I was very fearful of that. I didn't want to take the courses that show you all the stuff that goes on, and I was glad I didn't. I don't want to know about it. I was the best patient. I never had a problem, but I didn't want to know all those things. I just had a little bit of gas when I delivered. It wasn't as horrifying as I had expected it to be, let's put it that way, but it wasn't idealistic.

The "little bit of gas" left Linda unconscious during her first four deliveries, but she was able to watch her fifth, which she describes as fantastic.

Jerry was excited and supportive when she was pregnant. In keeping with their traditional division of labor, he was not in the delivery room for any of the births, and he did not help care for the newborns when they came home.

> The first six weeks were pretty much my thing. He has a fear of a newborn infant which is so, I think, for a lot of men. He's never bathed them as infants, not till they started to sit up.

Linda had no kin come to help after her children were born. She had no help after her first two and hired a woman for a week or two after the third, fourth, and fifth. In fact, starting when her first was an infant, she always had some regular outside help with her children.

> When I had Missy, I used to take like an afternoon, because our financial situation wasn't that great. When she was first born, I always had a teenager come like at 3:30 and would go out just for a couple of hours until 5:30. Then I worked myself into one day a week, and I've had Bonnie now for about four years. She comes at 8:30, and I leave until 3:30 when the children come home. She does everything. She cleans the kitchen and makes the beds, she does the wash and watches the kids. Of course, now it's nothing. Kimmy is home sometimes, but sometimes she'll just have the baby.
>
> I'd say Bonnie is about fifty-five. She is married and has no children, and she does volunteer work. She does this for a few families, friends of mine. She really loves doing it. She doesn't really vacuum or anything else. That's fine as far as I'm concerned; I want her to give all of her attention to my kids. If the baby is crying and she's got a load of wash to do, the baby comes first. But usually, because he's out playing or something, she'll have the time to manage it. She does the kitchen.
>
> And then I have teenagers; well, when it's necessary. In the summer I use them a lot, because I play tennis and swim, and I go to the beach. I have a teenager come and watch the baby. Like now this little girl across the street will take him for a walk for a half-hour in the afternoon.

This part-time paid childcare assistance enables Linda to relax, exercise, and socialize, in addition to tending to the needs of her large family. Although she and Jerry are both local, she has no mother and does not mention help from any other kin, during postpartum or day to day.

Linda disclaims any postpartum difficulties other than the confusion of the household. But particular children brought particular difficulties.

> The first one I think was hard because I was a new mother. I was the typical first mother. I called the pediatrician every day. So, consequently, when I think of Missy being a difficult child I can't say she was on her own, but because of my attitude she was. I mean I was a fool. It is amazing the kid ever turned out to be as normal as she is. I think your first child is always like that.
>
> All my babies were good; I think that's why I've had so many. They were all big babies, and they slept through the night right away. Brian, he's fantastic, but I've had more time for him. If I had to pick children, I'd say the second, third and fifth were the best.
>
> Kimmy, the fourth, was difficult and still is. She was the smallest [7.5 lbs.], and I think that had something to do with the feeding and all that. I think bigger babies are easier to handle. Kimmy was my independent child, anyway. She was like that from the beginning, when she was very independent and the most demanding, plus being fourth. Again, I'm sure I had less time for her. How do you determine whether it was her, or my lack of time for her and my impatience? There is a fine line between that.

Linda breastfed four of her infants, each for about six weeks.

> Six weeks was a good start for them. It was a good start for me, and it was convenient for those six weeks, and that was it. I did not nurse Kimmy because she was born in May, and we were going to the beach. I felt that it would be too difficult with all the children around and with all the neighbors sitting around and the kids coming over — my exposure would be so great. I felt that I didn't want to involve them in that.

That summer was a tough summer. I was at the beach, and I had just furnished the house. I had the two other little ones, and that was one of my most miserable summers. It was wonderful because we were at the beach, but emotionally it was tough because I had a lot to do. I love the beach, and I was somewhat restricted and stuff. I think it was really just motherhood in general.

Linda enjoys caring for babies.

I love babies: their softness, and they are so dependent, and their smell. They have that sweet aroma which permeates everything in the house. And I like everything that they do. The first smile: it's such a thrill, that smile. And when they keep their eyes open — I like all of it. There are times when their crankiness comes in and all that and it's annoying and you think, "Oh, no." But my babies have not been that much of crybabies. Of course, you put a pacifier in it's face, and you have so many kids that after each one there was always somebody there to go and pat their bottoms, that kind of thing. They are never long without attention.

Although Jerry does not help care for babies, he takes an active role with the children and helps around the house.

First of all, I don't manage the family alone. It is definitely a joint endeavor. We do it together. Usually what we do is we both get up at seven. He gets up before me sometimes. Jerry will come downstairs and start breakfast, and I sort of get up and make sure the kids are all getting dressed, and I have the baby, so I get him organized. I come down, and he's all set. Jerry makes the lunches. I usually don't do any bed-making or anything like that. I'm not that good in the morning. Jerry is our morning person, so he's good at that. He takes care of us, and we're usually around the breakfast table together. He makes waffles, cereal, English muffins. If there's bacon and eggs or anything I make that, but usually he'll make scrambled eggs. Sometimes I make corn muffins. My kids leave for school at 8:05.

Three days a week Kimmy goes to nursery school. Jerry takes her there on his way to the office. I have a friend whose little boy goes, and so Jerry picks him up, drops them off, and goes on his way. My friend picks them up — I just have to pick Kimmy up on Wednesdays.

He'll fill the dishwasher and clean the kitchen. He's never made a bed. He doesn't do wash. No, he has. Like when I just came home from the hospital or something, he'd throw a load of wash in, but not a regular basis, no. Clean the kitchen, that's his big thing. He doesn't wash the floor or anything like that. He'll put the dishes in the dishwasher, clean the stove, stuff like that. He might do it three times a week because my girls clean the kitchen. He'll maybe sweep the family room or something. He doesn't clean the bathroom. He has vacuumed a few times.

Jerry does the shopping. He knows what I need, and I give him my extra things. After twelve years of marriage, he sort of knows the basics. He gets the basics. Like if I'm going to make a dish with mushrooms, he doesn't buy those little gourmet kinds of things, those frivolous things. But he has a routine. About five years ago, or maybe longer than that, he started something with the children because we had all the girls, and I'm such a key figure in their lives, and he works all day. We sort of tried to get things to do with him. You know, they play dolls, and they want to bake with me. I do a lot of baking. So every Friday night he takes one of them with him out to dinner, to do the shopping, and then they go for ice cream.

It's adorable. And I'll tell you, those girls know whose turn it is. You have your choice to go where you want. It's usually Friendly's. It's really a big spot. He always takes them to get ice cream, and then they go and they do some grocery shopping. And they talk. It's absolutely beautiful. All our friends know about it because the kids are so delighted with it.

Linda appreciates Jerry's help but still considers home and child care to be her responsibility. While most of the mothers I spoke with who gave up their jobs to care for their children miss the activity and sociability of employment, Linda is one of the few who proudly focuses on the importance of her work at home.[3] Linda has a beautiful and enormous house including five bedrooms, living room, dining room, kitchen, family room, and a gorgeous patio room filled with plants. Three of her children are in public school; her fourth is in nursery school; her fifth is home.

On Kimmy's school days [Monday, Wednesday, Friday, 9-11:30 A.M.] it's just me and the baby. When she leaves, the baby is still up. I get him cleaned up and clean the kitchen at the same time. I do that together, and then I put him to bed. Today I put him in at 9:30 and that's usually the same. I do the kitchen, then I do that. Then I shower, exercise, and get dressed. Then I do my hair and my makeup. Then I make the beds. I'm upstairs and so I do upstairs: clean the bathrooms, make the beds. Then I finish cleaning up the kitchen, then I go around and make sure everything's straightened, like I go in the family room and straighten that all up. The kids are in charge of putting away their own toys, so, hopefully, that is done. I go through the whole house and straighten it up, so that it always looks presentable. It's not clean, but it's done. Then, depending on what time I have, I go and do whatever has to be done. If I have to vacuum, well, then I vacuum. If I have to wash the kitchen floor, then I do that. Once I have the house in good condition — all cleaned up, picked up, present- able — then I go about taking the furniture polish and I do that for as long as I can. I just keep going.

In between I go down and throw a load of wash in; I have at least a couple of loads a day. Sometimes I don't wash and then I have three or four loads. If I let it go for a day or two, which I can — it isn't so much the wash — what's taking it out and throwing it in? — but folding it. I have a table down there and there are mounds of it. I fold it down there and I pile it in each child's pile and they go down and get their own. But I'm not one for making my kids do the wash and stuff.

Somebody might call, and I might be in a conversation for twenty minutes, and then I get up and finish dusting or some- thing. If I'm really into something heavy I'll just say I can't talk, but if I feel like having a cigarette or sitting down, I will. It takes me a couple of hours to do this patio because by the time I water and trim everything, then I have to sweep the floor because stuff's all over the floor. It takes me about a week to get everything in order.

I don't have cleaning help. I did have a lady for two years in my other house after I had Kimmy. When Kimmy went to school I stopped having her. I had her once a week and that got the big things done. I feel like now I can handle it myself. I don't mind it. There are days when I get fed-up, but when you are on top of it it's not bad. I get a little overwhelmed every once in a while, and it sort of does get you down in a way. But as long as you keep up with it and do a little bit each time, as long as you don't allow it to overwhelm you and you stay on top of the situation, then there's no need to be upset about it. I consider it my occupation. I take pride in my house, and so that to me is sort of my job to have it like that. I like to have it nice for Jerry.

Jerry is the breadwinner of the family. His work is demanding and requires that he participate in many social events, which sometimes keep him away from home during family hours. Linda does her best to fill in for his absence.

He's been away from the children this week, and so I feel like I have made an extra effort this week to pull things together and to make them less aware of the change in our life. I think when I have a baby, and I'm in bed, he does that for me. We each try. We always maintain that nucleus.

Linda's family is clearly the center of her life, but she has recreational activities outside her home as well. For a combination of business and social reasons, she and Jerry belong to two country clubs.

We both play tennis. We usually play separately but we do play together, too. I play every Tuesday, on my day off, with some girls. Doubles. I have been doing that since Christmas. Now I'll play whenever I can, depending on the weather. And we'll play when he's home and he has two hours in an afternoon. We'll bring the baby over to the club, and maybe we'll play tennis. We play pretty well together. We'll play if another couple comes or not. We play Scrabble and cards, just the two of us. We enjoy each other that way. We like to go out and eat. When we go out, we usually go out to eat. We get a lot of invitations for social things, parties; people invite us for dinner, and we entertain for dinner and that sort of thing.

I went back to school last year. I loved it. I was going to start to matriculate this year. I went in the summer during my pregnancy, and now I don't know if I'm going to sign up for this summer. I haven't made that decision yet, and I will probably go in September, and I will try to work it out. Albertus is very good about returning students. They make a big effort to help you, and, of course, I need everything, so I can really fit into any slot. If I need a Tuesday, there's always something offered on a Tuesday that I need. So I went back to school. I am creative. I like to knit and sew, and I make lots of things. I do a lot of that with the kids, making little things that they can put together. I'm involved with the church; that takes up a lot of my time. I bicycle. I used to bike ride every day when I was pregnant with Brian, right up to the end. I swim; I swim all summer. We take trips.

Linda feels that her marriage has improved with age.

Our marriage has gotten better in the twelve years. Let's say, more in the beginning, I would blame myself that I did not have as much control or as much maturity as I have now. I have a tendency to fly off the handle. I'd be very intense about a certain thing. I could scream at Jerry for half an hour, and Jerry would just sit there. He's that kind: very calm and easy- going. I didn't like it! There's nothing I like better than a good argument. But in the years that sort of has comeabout. Now I feel mature enough that we can sit down and discuss something, and really we don't always have the same opinion. We have differences, but it can be more conversive and quiet, and I try very hard to see his point of view, and he tries very hard to see mine. This is why our marriage has gotten to the stage that it has, because there is more give and take.

I have to say this. It has nothing to do with this but it has to do with me. I have become what I consider to be a born-again Christian a year and a half ago. And since this has taken place in my life, my attitudes have made me more aware of everyone's feelings and have helped me to be more Christian in my life in general. To me, that has made our marriage even better. And I know if Jerry had to say, I know that he would say the last two years I have much more respect, in general. I have that attitude, and it's certainly from becoming a born-again Christian.

He might say he has become born-again, but comparing himself to me it would be no. I have actually gone through a transition. Jerry is sweet; he's just a terrific guy. From day one when I met him until now, he has never changed. He's a wonderful person and anyone that knows Jerry says that. I don't think anyone who knows Jerry doesn't like him. I have not always been a wonderful person. I have made a big change in the past two years. I feel like I'm approaching wonderful, but it's definitely through my Christian feelings.

Linda alludes to marital tensions in the past and sees her marriage as benefiting from her change in faith. It also benefits from an annual income of $82,000 plus perquisites from Jerry's business.

We make enough money to do and have what we want. We belong to two clubs — that is the real extravagance, clubs. The people at the yacht club are very rich; it's a very rich club. We live there in the summer, and we have friends that belong there, so that we were finding ourselves there all the time as guests, and then Jerry started writing some business because of that club, and one of his friends who is a member wanted Jerry to join, and Jerry felt it would be good. It's not paid for by his business; we pay for it ourselves. We belong to the Quinnipiac Club, which is a very fine eating club. It's an elegant place. So we do these things, and I buy pretty much what I want. We do not have any financial stress, but we do live within boundaries.

The division of labor between Linda and Jerry is clear and traditional. He makes a good living; she cares for their large home and family. This is consistent with her expectations of what her life would be like, only better because their standard of living is high, especially in contrast with her childhood. Linda cannot imagine a life without children, or one that combines employment and motherhood.

I feel sorry for married women who choose not to have children, because I think they are missing a lot. I feel like there's no reason why you can't accomplish those things, although I do not believe in women who have small children going to work. I think that's wrong. I feel like if you want a family, why have a baby that's six weeks old and hire a woman five days a week and go to work? Now, if you have to do that, fine, if you didn't want that child to begin with, I suppose I could accept that. But I feel if that's the role that you have accepted in your life, then you should play the role out. Those mothers gone, leaving infants home while they work... to me, why have kids? I had my kids because I wanted to enjoy them. Having kids, for what? To me, that's to satisfy your ego when they grow up or something.

I'm not saying when they go to school. When the children go to school, like I was going back to school, and I fully intended on being a full-time student in September. But I was going to do that with Kimmy in school and in the hours that they were gone and that's it. I don't feel that you should leave them five days a week. I just can't agree with that. Wait five years.

I think that one regret that I have was that I did not get married younger to enjoy my children in those young years. I was mature and ready at twenty-five to settle down and have a family and that was fine for me, but in terms of physical childbearing and the whole bit, patience and playing with kids, I would have liked that extra five years. But again, it worked out fine for me, and I've managed beautifully.

And I was disappointed because I was going to matriculate in September, and I was really getting into this whole school thing. I got pregnant with Brian, and then I felt like, well, I'll go back, I'll take one course, I'll take two, and when he goes to school then I'll do it. My life is not ended because I'm pregnant or having babies or something else. I can wait. Women who do that have a tendency to feel like everything has got to be done in those years between twenty and thirty. It isn't true.

Linda's fifth pregnancy was an accident. Although she was "free and easy" about the timing of her first four pregnancies, she was using contraception by the time Brian was conceived. She was disappointed because she was enjoying taking college courses. At age thirty-seven, she struggles to resist feeling in a hurry.

> That's why I disagree with *Passages* in so many ways. She classifies you. When you're age thirty-five, then certain things are going to happen to you. I don't think that's true at all. I am a late maturer, so for me it's thirty-seven already and I feel like a girl who is twenty-seven.

Linda sees her future as perhaps including another pregnancy. It also includes college and, eventually, teaching.

> I'd say teaching is my ultimate goal. Even if I substituted, even if I did get a degree and was able to teach I could do substitute work. Or I could volunteer, something where I could make a difference.

Linda is happy with her choices. She perceives motherhood as having helped her develop as a person.

> Being a mother has given me more confidence, security, a sense of importance. I mean, I affect five people. I don't say simply that the children depend on me. I feel important. The love that's generated is fabulous. I am affectionate and loving and to have that response come back, to see that — because I think that babies respond to love — it's beautiful. For me as an individual — definitely security, more confidence, I'm more aware of my capabilities.
>
> I know if my mother were alive she would never believe that I would ever have had five kids—I was always afraid of being in the hospital, I was never really sick, and then I had all the kids like a snap, and I always think of my mother. She always said, "Oh, Linda, she'll never be able to deal with kids and all this and that," but I did well with all the kids. I think she'd be surprised. I've surprised myself.

Linda had limited options while growing up. Her working-class family could provide few financial or educational resources and had no expectations that Linda would achieve outside the realm of the family. Her mother even communicated some doubt that Linda would be able to cope with having and caring for children. In the context of these prospects, Linda feels very successful. She has a good marriage and five healthy children; she is a good wife and mother. She lives well, much better than her parents ever did. These accomplishments provide her with obvious satisfaction.

Her upper-middle-class marriage has, in fact, opened up opportunities that she never had before. Linda is now seeking additional avenues to self-actualization. She wants to attend college. She wants to be a teacher. These are her goals for the next fifteen years. Her plans for herself have been frustrated by her unexpected fifth pregnancy, yet she maintains her strong commitment to full-time mothering. Already in her late thirties, she needs time for her own pursuits, yet she has a new infant. She has turned to religion to help her be a nicer person, to help her be patient with the needs of others. Her conflict surfaces in her wish that she had started her family sooner. Having neither done that, nor pursued her own education in her early twenties, it takes effort to resist the pressure she now feels. Her commitment to full-time motherhood was not an active choice; she perceived no other options. Now, after eleven years of motherhood, she shows signs of strain, strain which she feels she has learned to control by becoming a born-again Christian.

5

Nina

I'm pretty much as I was before.

Nina is from a large, local working-class family similar to Linda's, but her inclinations and choices have been consistently different from Linda's. Perhaps because she was the oldest rather than the youngest child, she was aware of the difficulties in her mother's life and was in no rush to get married or have a family. Nina always wanted to be "something" when she grew up. When her mother's friend offered financial assistance for college, Nina jumped at the chance. Some years later she earned her master's degree in teaching. Since that time she has taught almost continuously, sometimes full time, sometimes part time.

Nina met her husband, Jim, in the Peace Corps. They had been married four years and had lived in several locations when she decided it was time to have a child. Although Jim was reluctant to become a father, when the baby arrived he became an active, caretaking parent.

Nina is a mother of two who is employed as a part-time teacher while actively seeking a full-time position. She feels that having children has slowed down her career, but not altered its direction or her commitment.

Her conjugal relationship, based upon shared roles, enables her to enjoy both family and employment. Jim shares responsibility for childcare and household maintenance; he shops and cooks and cleans and transports the kids at least as much as Nina does.

Nina has formed a marriage and a family quite unlike the one in which she was raised. She moved away from home to go to school and stayed away many years. When she returned to her old locale she had a husband, a profession, and a child. She enjoys the support of having her siblings and high school friends nearby, but continues to live differently from the way her parents did.

❦ ❦ ❦

I think I wanted to be lots of things at different times: cowgirl, veterinarian, archeologist, artist — depends when. I was not particularly interested in marriage. I suppose I imagined I would be married, but my mother wasn't married until she was twenty-eight, and there was certainly no parental push that this is what I should be thinking about at any point in my life.

Perhaps as a very young child I wanted to be a mother; I don't recall. As a teenager, I had babies — I mean my mother had. I was something like fourteen when my younger sister was born, so I was quite aware of how difficult it was for my mother to have these children so late in her life. She was forty-three when my younger sister was born.

Nina was the oldest of five children, four girls and one boy. She grew up in southern New England, where her mother had also been born and raised. Until Nina was ten, her family lived with her mother's brother in a small converted cottage on her maternal grandfather's property. Her father and mother worked in a factory; a babysitter came in to care for the children. This living arrangement created tension between her parents.

As a young child my father wasn't home that much. He worked in a factory, and he came home. He was not particularly happy with the living situation. He drank a great deal, but he was never brutal to us children at all. But I wouldn't see much of him. As we became older, he seemed to be home more. He was very authoritarian.

When Nina was ten, her grandfather committed suicide. Her parents' share of his estate enabled them to buy a home in a neighboring town. Soon after, her father opened a catering business, and her mother began to prepare food in their home for his business. These changes, however, did not make her father content.

> I always felt his major weakness was his inability to be satisfied with what he had, a devoted wife and five kids. He was never a family man, isn't to this day. He'd much prefer to play cards all night with his boyfriends and go to the racetrack.

Nina's childhood memories are quite mixed. There was the fun of extended family and the pain of her parents' unhappy marriage.

> We had a lovely yard. Often my cousins, aunts, and uncles would come and we'd have fun playing ghost. And I had a place nearby where we could play with my friends. We never roamed very far.
> My father didn't particularly enjoy doing things with the family. I can remember very vividly going on one picnic with him. It was very unpleasant.
> As a young child, I think I was aware that things were not perfect as far as my parents were concerned. And certainly as an adolescent I was acutely aware of the fact that, from my mother's point of view, the marriage was a very unhealthy one.

Nina was very close to her mother.

> We could talk about so many things. She was very vibrant and liked to do things. We did everything from painting the house, to gardening, to cooking. She'd sew — I never did sew.

Both of Nina's parents had high school diplomas. Nina was a good student and aspired to a career, although she was not sure in what field. She went away to college, enabled by a scholarship she earned and financial assistance from her mother's best friend. Although three of her siblings tried college, Nina is the only one in the family to have earned her degree. After graduation from college she joined the Peace Corps.

Nina met Jim in the Peace Corps.

We were in training for three months, and I didn't know him. When we got to Panama, I met him, and we were married a year later. It was a very strong physical attraction. It was a very tumultuous courtship, up and down. I mean I was in love with him very much; they were very happy times. We had a lot of time, and we were free of responsibilities and free of parental pressures which were later very great.

Parental pressure began around their wedding.

Our families met. My husband is from New York so his mother invited my parents. Then my parents had come to Panama to visit, and then both families came for our wedding — but my father didn't attend.

It was extremely complicated. Jim's father was Irish, and his mother was Jewish. He, in turn, wanted to be baptized. He was baptized Catholic. My other problem was that my father wasn't Catholic, although I was raised Catholic. A friend of ours had been married in, again, a mixed situation and was married by the Justice of the Peace, and I definitely didn't want that. Because we were both nominally Catholic, we decided we would have a Catholic wedding. All was well until about two days before the wedding, the day before my parents were to arrive. We were asked to sign a paper saying that we would practice the church's teachings about birth control. Impossible! And that was that — we weren't married in a Catholic church, and my father refused to come.

I had already told my husband things about my father, and he said well, he could understand my father's point of view. And when my parents had come to Panama, he was very impressed with my father. But after this episode, my husband had had it with my father.

Nina and Jim spent their first six months of married life in the Peace Corps and then returned to the States, locating in Washington, D.C. Several months after their return, Nina's mother committed suicide. This delayed Nina's entrance to graduate school.

> Jim went into an urban teaching project. I had found the Peace Corps very disillusioning in many ways, and I wasn't about to jump into the ghetto and do nice things without knowing anything. I sort of slept and watched television for about four months. Then I worked in Lord and Taylor during the Christmas rush, and then I worked in the business office of *National Geographic*. Then that May my mother died, and we came up here to Connecticut for the summer.
> Then I went into the Master's in Teaching program. It took me two years to get my master's because I entered a quarter late. I was an intern for one year in a high school, and then they hired me, and I taught full time that second year and was also sort of a student part time. I got my MAT at the end of that year. Roger was born that August, and we moved to Puerto Rico.

Jim strongly supported Nina's career development. Nonetheless, at times she felt tension about their both being in the field of teaching.

> I think it was up and down, good and bad. I think that from my point of view, though, he certainly was very encouraging about my going to school. I think the fact that we were in the same career has been difficult at times. I think at times he's felt threatened by sort of a personality thing, I suppose. At least for part of the time I think it's true; a good part of the time I was much happier with my situation than he was with his, and I made a lot more friends, but I think that's a function of an awful lot of strong women teaching at our level.

At the time of the interviews, Nina and Jim were both thirty-six years old. Their son Roger was almost nine, their daughter Becky was five. Nina taught English as a Second Language five mornings a week, Jim was a public school teacher, Roger attended private school, and Becky attended morning nursery school.

Nina and Jim were not in accord about having a child. When Nina was ready, Jim was ambivalent.

Well, we had talked about it. I was twenty-six and I felt that if I were going to have children — and I couldn't conceive of not having them — now was the time. He was initially unhappy. I think it was just the idea that he had that he was going to be faced with tremendous responsibilities. I was pregnant, and he was unhappy, but that did not last very long. From day one that we have had both of the children, he has adored them.

Nina felt pressure to have a child.

I don't know the specific individuals, but I felt that certain societal push that gee, here I was twenty-six and married four years. I was using the pill. I would read articles and get all upset about it, and I stopped taking it. Well, we didn't say, "Okay, now we are going to have kids" — I don't know if we ever verbalized it.

I think having a child may have improved our marriage. It is really difficult to say. It didn't cause an incredible change in our relationship. I certainly think that it had a sobering effect on both of us. We had really been terribly free, and we had traveled a great deal, and we were unconcerned about money and how we lived and did as we wished, pretty much. That is normal. The baby affected things considerably, although we still traveled a great deal.

Nina worked during her first pregnancy. Like Elizabeth and other mobile women with careers, she was not enchanted with pregnancy but took it in stride.

I kept working. I didn't particularly enjoy being pregnant, I mean it wasn't the highlight of my life, but I didn't have problems. I was healthy. I was happy, in both cases, about having another child, and if this was the means to an end then okay. There were little problems with both deliveries, which upset me a great deal, but nothing major.

Jim didn't get that involved in the first pregnancy. He and Nina did not take childbirth classes.

I wasn't scared of giving birth the first time, but I was scared afterwards. I did prepare for childbirth the second time — we went to Lamaze classes.

The hospital experience definitely frightened me. The labor pains were much greater than I had anticipated, and my doctor was out of town. I had to go to a different hospital. The nurse examined me and told me it was going to be hours before I had the baby. Then they gave me a shot of pitocin, and the baby was born in a matter of hours — very, very quickly — and I was anesthetized, which I didn't want to be. At the point she told me it was necessary, she could have said I have to cut off your leg, and I would have agreed. I had gas. I was not conscious. I never saw the doctor; I don't think he delivered Roger.

Almost the same exact thing happened to me the second time, which caused me considerable anger. I got in there, and again my water had broken at about six that morning. I went to my doctor at ten, and he said, "Your cervix is absolutely tight. Go home. There is no point in your going into the hospital and being charged for a day of waiting."

Finally labor did begin, and it seemed to me the contractions were strong and close together, and I went to the hospital. When the resident examined me, he called my doctor and told him not to come — I definitely was not going to give birth that soon. So the resident said, "Hook her up to the pitocin," and again things happened very quickly. The signals I was getting were very confusing to me. The nurse would be saying, "Oh, you're in the huffy-puffy stage already," and the resident comes in and turns up the machine. She subsequently turned it down. Well, anyway, my doctor came and I was given a local anesthetic again [peridural]. I agreed to it because I was very confused. And then the nurse said to me, "If you had waited, the baby would have been born in five minutes," but that was the first positive sign I had had from her that anything was really happening. And the baby was born. She was born within three hours, and I was told it was going to be six to ten. I was very upset about Roger's experience, and I thought this was going to be very different, but, as I say, it turned out to be exactly the same thing.

Although the circumstances were not actually "exactly the same," what remains with Nina is the feeling that things went wrong both times. She was not in control; communication with the hospital staff was confusing and medical intervention made it hard for her to understand her own labor; she was unable to deliver without anesthetic as she had wished. Unlike when she delivered Roger, however, she was awake when Becky was born and Jim was with her.

> Forceps were used for both deliveries. I don't know what the cause was with her. With him, the doctor was just in a rush; he had surgery in an hour and a half.

When Nina had Roger, she and Jim were mobile. Nina's mother was not living, so her sister came to help for the week after she came home from the hospital. For mobile women, this brief, full-time assistance was typical. After Becky, Nina was again local.

> Maybe my sister took Roger during the day or something, I don't really recall.

For local women, this less formal assistance predominated and was likely to last indefinitely.

> In both instances I was very tired — exhausted. And my mother, after she gave birth, was home a day and then was up doing everything!
> Jim, from the very beginning, was extremely helpful. The first night Roger came home — I breastfed Becky but not Roger — I got up in the middle of the night, and he woke up, and I started feeding the baby, but I could tell the way he was looking he wanted to do it. I said, "Do you want to do it?" and he said, "Yes," and he did it.

Nina, who planned to be employed after Roger was born, had, with Jim, chosen to relocate to a place where childcare arrangements would be easy to make.

We had taken the job with the understanding that there would be no problem in getting a babysitter, someone to come in and stay with the baby. As it turned out, when we got to Puerto Rico we couldn't find a babysitter. So Jim went to work and I stayed home — for how many weeks? — not long.

We were in agreement that we were going to leave the baby with a babysitter; we were very concerned about it. If anything, he more than I. One reason we moved there was because I just couldn't stand the suburbs, and I wanted to move to Puerto Rico to get away from it. We ended up in what they call Burke Houses. But it was nice because we had this woman right next door to us who was like a super-mother type. She loved babies; she was so concerned about Roger and always listening for him while we were working. We thought it was marvelous to have the house so close — suddenly this became very advantageous.

Because of the move, Nina chose not to breastfeed Roger.

I moved to Puerto Rico when he was seventeen days old. I was going back to work immediately. I felt, and I kept reading, that one should be relaxed, and I was pretty relaxed, but I didn't feel I was relaxed enough.

Nina did nurse Becky, but did not particularly like it and stopped after three months.

I found it a big disadvantage — Jim had done so much with Roger, getting up in the night and so forth and, also, she was gaining very, very slowly. It seemed to be of some concern to the doctor, and it was a concern of mine as well. It was primarily for my own convenience, but I was also at a point where I was not convinced that it was in her best interest to continue. I felt it was easier for me to handfeed her the bottle.

The transition to parenthood was not difficult for Nina. As oldest of five she had had a great deal of experience with babies, her babies weren't difficult, and her husband shared infant care. In addition, she continued to work.[1]

> When I was pregnant with Roger we were living in Washington, D.C. I wanted to continue to work. I thought it would be easier to continue to teach in Puerto Rico. I had a babysitter who came in for him. After we were heading for the third babysitter, it was too much of a strain on us. My husband stayed home for one and a half years with Roger, and I continued to work.

Jim is the only mate of the women with whom I spoke who stayed home for a period to be primary caretaker of the children. He and Nina clearly share responsibility for child and home care. Only four of the thirty mates share responsibility; in all cases the mother, like Nina, is employed.

When Nina and Jim returned to the States, it was her turn to be home with Roger.

> When we moved back to the States from Puerto Rico, the idea of putting Roger into a daycare center, or anything like that, just was not something we would consider. I don't even know if there were any. At that time, I just did not feel that he should be, as a young child, removed from the home. I could have gotten a babysitter to come in, but finances entered into this, and it just seemed more reasonable at that time for one of us to take care of him and one to work.
>
> Had I continued to teach then, I would be teaching right now. There were opportunities to get jobs seven years ago, but there are not at the moment.

Nina was happy to have a child, but was not crazy about infant care.

> I liked infant care to a point. I liked to watch — they develop so rapidly... and changes — seeing them every day. But generally I found I preferred them much more when they started talking and saying something new every day.

The decision to have a second child was no easier for Nina and Jim than the first had been.

It was difficult for us. My husband was not anxious to have two children because he realized, having spent as much time as he did with our first, that it really is a lot of work. He was more reluctant than I; I just could not conceive of having just one child at that time. I was thirty when I had Becky, and I felt that if I were going to have any more children I had to have them on or before I was thirty, and I just made it.

Also, we were settled. We had been traveling a great deal and things were very uncertain as to what Jim would be doing, what I would be doing, where we would be living. When we came to New Haven, it was apparent that we would be here for some time. That, too, was a factor.

Jim certainly did not want any more than two children.

He had a vasectomy while I was pregnant with Becky.

After Becky was born, Nina stayed home with her for a year and then worked part time.

I worked but I worked on a schedule where I went in at three, when Jim came home. That I think was for a year. At two, she went to daycare. She was two in May, and she went into daycare in September. She stayed there from September until May and then went to nursery school.

Family responsibilities continue to be shared by Nina and Jim.

Jim usually gets up earlier then the rest of us. He gets up and runs six to ten miles. Then both of us do what needs to be done; it depends upon the day. Now, this morning I said something about lunch and he said, "I already made it." I was about to make it.

During the week they eat cereal and sometimes they'll have a banana on the cereal. Sometimes I'll make eggs for them. All winter they had only cocoa and toast for breakfast, if that. So there's not much to supervise. I have my breakfast. I have a very relaxed breakfast and coffee and I read the newspapers quickly.

Roger and Becky may watch television. Jim's taking his shower, and then he runs around and does the chores that he set up for himself. Then Roger is supposed to be at school at twenty-five after eight, so he and Roger leave here about eight-thirty in the morning. It's driving me crazy because I am compulsively punctual.

I am left with Becky. We leave the house at quarter to nine. She has to be at nursery school at nine. I start work at nine-thirty. We're supposed to be there at nine-fifteen; I'm usually there about nine. I pick her up at noon.

Roger gets out at three-fifteen. Jim picks him up on Mondays and Wednesdays. I pick him up on Tuesdays, Thursdays, and Fridays. He gets out at twelve-fifteen on Fridays. Jim is involved with something on Tuesdays and Thursdays, although this winter he was picking him up every day but Friday.

In the beginning of the year, I taught three nights a week as well as five mornings. Jim did a lot of the cooking the nights that I worked, but, as it stands now, I do most of the cooking. We're not gourmet cooks during the week.

It varies — there are some weeks I don't cook, and there are some weeks he doesn't cook. I would say it's generally fifty-fifty. We discuss meals. We talk about it together. We'll have chicken tonight, and there's a special on hamburger tomorrow, so we'll have hamburger. He goes to the market. He washes the dinner dishes most of the time. I wash the breakfast and lunch dishes. We don't have a dishwasher. He does most of the cleaning, but we have worked something out, and we have a student come from Southern once a week, and now we have a woman coming tomorrow, not a student, someone else recommended for us for a few hours a week to vacuum, clean the bathroom, dust.

Nina does not consider herself primary caretaker; both she and Jim are equally involved with the children. Their styles are somewhat different, but the differences cause little conflict.

I am more authoritarian than Jim. He just doesn't get upset about much of anything; I think he thinks a lot of things are very amusing. I also think — he may agree or disagree — that his children just can do no wrong.

We operate independently, but I think the fact that we are still married and have these kids together means we have obviously agreed on pretty much, because we spend a great deal of time together, and we spend a great deal of time with the children.

Roger is extremely close to his father, as is Becky. I'm very happy that it is the way it is. He's very happy being with the children as much as he is, and I'm happy that he's with them, and that gives me considerably more leeway.

Nina stresses how much flexibility she feels she has because of Jim's active participation in caring for the children. In contrast to her mother and to other women she knows, Nina feels that having children has not limited her life.

I think of Jim and the role he has played in bringing up our children. I would say fifty-fifty, maybe sixty-forty. He has given me a great deal of freedom and flexibility.

I think I'm pretty much as I was before I had the children. Having a husband who is supportive in bringing them up hasn't forced me to really give things up — not that we don't tear apart together over certain things. And they've been easy children to raise; they've been healthy children.

Yet, she wishes she were teaching full time. She blames the job market, not the needs of her family, for her difficulty getting full-time employment.

I would take a full-time job tomorrow. I have applications in.

Their only sources of income are their two jobs. She earns about nine thousand and he thirty thousand dollars a year. Meeting the financial needs of their family of four requires careful budgeting, especially with private school tuitions to pay.

Jim has been taking care of the money for a long time. When I was home and he was working I used to, but now he pays the bills. I don't quite understand his system. I would say we are on a budget of sorts. He allots so much money for the weekends, so much money for food, etc.

We have a joint account. He has a separate account and he has encouraged me for a long time to open a separate account, but I just haven't.

I'm only paid once a month; he's paid twice a month. When my check comes, he divides it four ways: one hundred dollars towards our mortgage, and the remainder is divided three ways: one-third goes into Roger's account, one-third in Becky's, and the rest is mine to get me through the month. But he doesn't want me to use it for gas and so forth. It's if I want to buy a new tree for the yard.

Out of each of his checks, he takes our bills. He doesn't pay the gas bill in one. Out of his bigger check — one check has more deductions than the other — the bigger one he'll take out so much towards the gas, so much for the phone company. We have big gas bills because we are heated with gas and everything is gas. So that gets paid with two checks. The others, the bigger checks, are the main bills. The two credit cards we happen to have, we pay so much on them and on the mortgage. It is a crazy bookkeeping system. It's his system, and it works for him. I would do it differently.

What goes in his account is any extra money. If his aunt sends him one hundred dollars for his birthday, he puts it in his account, hoping to buy a new pair of... whatever.

The money is put into the children's accounts to pay their private school tuitions. It's in and out, in and out. Their grandparents send them a thousand dollars a year. One thousand for two children in private school is a drop in the bucket — but it helps.

Being short on money limits Nina and Jim's recreational choices. For example, they used to go to the movies a lot.

We used to but we find ourselves, especially when I'm working, just happy to be home. And we find it's very expensive for us to go, even for me. That doesn't stop us if there's a great movie, but there aren't many.

Prior to this year we had gone out in the evening at least once a week. It's been less than that this year. But we have committed ourselves, at least for another year, to private school tuitions.

Nina misses travel.

We like to travel. We said that was something we could do with one, but it is not as easy to do with two. If we had more money, I think we'd travel more. We travel very little right now. Although we got excited when someone told us there is a round-trip excursion fare to England for only four hundred eighty-three dollars.

Nina does have recreational activities.

I like reading, movies, music, running. I'd like to do more of that. Jim runs a lot, plays rugby in the fall and in the spring, reads constantly, plays with the children. In the summer we belong to the Y lake, and we all go there.

Although Nina is very family-oriented, she, like other women with careers, does not feel home-centered.

I never know my neighbors. This is the roof over my head, a place for the kids to play in, that's the way I look upon it. My contact with the neighbors is just through the children. If there is a problem, I send Jim out — I don't deal with it. I tend to have a much shorter fuse than he has about things like that.

My friends are people I work with and people I have met through the children, because when I came back to New Haven the contacts I had with other women were women who were taking their children to nursery school. I have one high school friend who has been my friend for years. We are very close.

Nina's father and all her sisters and brothers are close by. Although she does not see them often, she knows she can count on them.

> I see my father about three times a year. In a good year two times. My sister lives very close. She happened to be here today, but she doesn't come by that often. I talk to them often on the phone, but I don't see them that often.

Nina established her adult patterns during her first six years of married life, when she was mobile. Most of her social contacts in her hometown are with new friends. But like other local women, Nina has a rich network of social resources to call upon, if needed.

> If I needed help during a crisis, I would probably call on my sister because her child is in school full time, and she's not working, so it would be the least imposition. When I need a babysitter, I call this high school friend of mine who has four kids and is always willing to take Becky and is very nice about it. But I don't feel I could use her endlessly either because she has quite a handful.

She has, perhaps, the best of both the mobile and the local patterns: a spouse who shares responsibility for child and home care, and a network of kin and friends upon whom she can call if necessary. Because of Jim's sharing of roles, the necessity of calling on her kin arises infrequently, but they are there for her.

Nina wants a lot for her children.

> I want them to have every opportunity to learn about themselves, to learn about other people. At this point, I want them to have a happy childhood — and it's difficult in the times in which we live to keep this in perspective. He's only eight years old, give him a break. But I also think, given the nature of the world in which we live, I want them to be prepared—as best Jim and I are able to do it — to be able to cope with the world as they are going to find it.

I think childrearing has been a very exciting and, up to now, good and happy experience. I can imagine not having had children. I think if Jim and I were married I would be working full time and we would be traveling more. But I'm not envious of that.

Nina sees her future as including full-time employment. Asked about her expectations for her life in fifteen years, employment is her main issue.

I expect to be working full time in...I don't know...teaching. I would like to teach. It's something I've enjoyed very much but, given what the job market is, it might be something else. I just don't know. I'm sure I will be working in some capacity.

Nina's desire to "be something," her academic success, and a lucky opportunity enabled her to go off to college and escape the limited options that are the fate of many working-class girls. She married a middle-class man who encouraged her to prepare for a career and who supports, in both word and deed, her plan to combine motherhood and employment. Their conjugal relationship is based upon shared roles and respect for each other's work. While Nina's career has suffered because she reduced her employment to part time when her second child was an infant and has subsequently been unable to find a full-time position, she blames that on the job market and not on motherhood. While she would be happier if she had been able to resume full-time teaching when she had planned, she is content with her choices.

6

Pam

It seemed a shame to pass motherhood by.

Pam, like Elizabeth, is the career-oriented only child of a
middle-class, widowed parent. Their similarities do not end
there. As a child, Pam also wanted to be something adventurous, not a suburban housewife and mother. Unlike most of the
kids in her southern town, she went off to college, eager to get
away from home. She was raised by her mother; her father died
when she was eight.

Pam graduated from college, taught for a few years far from
home, then returned to school to earn her master's degree.
Although she did not rule out marriage, her somewhat negative
view of the institution led her to place more emphasis on
pursuing a career. She met Marty in graduate school and, "because he was really special," married him about a year later.
When she decided to marry she shaped her career choices to
suit the geographical mobility that Marty's scientific career
would require. Although she found work wherever they
moved, her job changes were always parallel; she never progressed up the professional ladder.

After three years of marriage, Pam and Marty decided to
have a child. Although Marty was open to her continuing to
work, she chose to be a full-time mother and homemaker. After
one year at home, however, Marty feared she was going to go
crazy and encouraged her to return to work part time. This she
happily did and, except for brief breaks due to the illness and
death of her mother and a second pregnancy, continues to teach
two evenings a week. When I spoke to her she expected to

deliver twins in two weeks but planned to return to her job next semester.

Their conjugal relationship changed a lot as a result of having a child. Originally they were like friends and lovers rather than spouses. When the baby came along their division of labor became more traditional. Pam strove to be "super" wife and mother, but it wore her down. Consequently, Marty has become more sensitive to the needs of the household and helps with more of the housework and childcare, and Pam has realized she needs to continue working part time.

Pam is a woman with career commitment, which she has put on hold while her family is young. Although she maintains contact with her profession by teaching two nights a week, she is a full-time homemaker. Most of the mothers with career commitment, like Elizabeth and Nina, have fuller employment; Pam is one of only two who do not. She looks forward to resuming her career full time when the twins are in school, although she knows she might not be able to wait that long.

❧ ❧ ❧

I didn't want to be a suburban housewife; I didn't want to get married; I didn't want to have children. From about the 10th grade on, I wanted to work in an embassy in another country. I always wanted to be something very adventurous. I didn't want to stay in my hometown, and I didn't want to marry someone who went to the apprentice school and worked in the shipyard.

My hometown is primarily a blue-collar community with most of the people working in the shipyard. A lot of boys who probably should have gone to college went to the apprentice school, which is part of the shipyard, instead. They go for four years. They get a two-year degree and training as an electrician or something like that. And most of the people are still there. When I go back, most of my high school friends are still there.

I really didn't go to college to be something great; I went to college because I wanted to get away from home. It wasn't until I really got into college that I had any understanding of what college was. I think I was the only one who never felt homesick. I was very much ready to get away from home and be on my own.

Pam grew up in a middle-class environment in the South. She was an only child, adopted when her mother was forty-one and her father was fifty-two. Pam's father owned a coalyard. He died when she was eight years old. Pam's mother was a homemaker until, when Pam was twelve, she took a job as a drugstore clerk. When Pam went off to college her mother became the secretary for an elementary school. Her mother was a strong role model.

You must realize that I was raised by someone who was left alone with an eight-year-old child. So even though she was a very typical housewife, by the very nature of the fact that she cooked so well and did things so well, I had a much stronger sense of what a woman could do and much fewer limits on me than a family where the man had always been the one you turned to. I was accustomed to having an example. I mean she shuddered — she didn't like having this influence. She always told me if my father were alive I wouldn't be doing these things, which was probably true. The example of her making decisions and taking control of her life, I am sure, had a great influence on me not being afraid to cope with life outside a very father-oriented family.

After college graduation, Pam moved to the west coast and took a teaching job. She spent three years in the singles scene, which initially seemed more attractive than marriage.

When I was in San Francisco I saw people being on merry-go-rounds. I was twenty-two, and they were in their thirties, and they were doing the same thing that I was doing, which was teaching and partying and getting involved in various relationships which always ended in some sort of strange way. I decided that this life — I mean I had competition between roommates as to who could have the most experiences this month, who could get a guy to take them to the most expensive restaurant — was really horrible! Anyway, it wasn't as it was on the ads on TV. All of us were from small towns who had been lured in some ways into thinking that there was this other life that was so much more sublime, and during those three years I think I came to appreciate the fact that they were not the values that I wanted. So I went back to North Carolina to graduate school, knowing that I really did want to do something that was personally rewarding to me. Marriage at that point was nothing: it wasn't negative, it wasn't positive. When I went back I felt that if I met someone who I really saw could add to a relationship, it would be a good relationship; I didn't feel negative about the whole institution. Yet, I didn't feel that it was necessarily something that was important that I have in order to be happy.

I realized marriage didn't have to be quite so boring as I thought it was when I was younger. But I also realized that it could be much worse than I ever conceived of it being, were I not married to someone with whom I could get along. It bothered me a great deal that I found myself to be quite boring sometimes, especially when I was tired or something, and that when you got married you wouldn't be the livewire but this person would find out how inadequate you were. So I felt that whatever relationship I entered into with a guy would be one in which I could go out with dirty hair at times and run into on a casual basis, that there was no way I could tell whether I wanted to marry someone or not on just a sort of dating-on-the-weekends basis.

By the time she met Marty in graduate school, Pam had dated a lot. She had already had three serious relationships.

I probably needed more experience to be able to understand men than someone who had been raised with a father. Most of them I found rather inadequate.

Marty hadn't dated very much, and he wasn't cool, and he didn't try to impress me. He was comfortable being himself, yet he wasn't comfortable in a sort of showing-off role. I dated a lot of guys who were fairly sophisticated, or thought they were. He didn't feel a need to make me any different or to subordinate me. I tended to be more independent than a lot of guys I dated liked because I hadn't been raised listening to a man. They spent an awful lot of time trying to make me into a slightly different person, and he didn't have as many prejudices as they did. He just sort of accepted people, and so I was able to grow in the relationship without feeling trapped.

He asked me if I would marry him in June. We had met in September. It was obviously a rather shocking thought to me because I went into the bathroom and threw up. After which I said, "Yes, I think so." We got married in August. If we had waited, I'm sure I would have chickened out, but I'm glad I didn't. I felt both happy and scared. I felt marriage was a very serious thing, and already, by that time, a lot of people that I knew in high school and college were getting divorces, and I felt sort of frightened but excited. Normal feelings, I think, but a bit less giddy than if I had been younger.

The decision to marry Marty altered Pam's career plans from career only to career and marriage.

I had accepted a job to administer a reading program in a local county, but didn't sign the contract. Shortly thereafter Marty and I decided to get married, so I changed my mind and taught. He had one year of graduate school left. I made a conscious decision at that point not to put the pursuit of my career first. I decided that he was special. After he got his degree, like all scientists, we have been totally at the mercy of society ever since.

At the time that we spoke, Pam and Marty had been married nine years, and Marty's career had taken them to four different locations.

I've been very lucky in getting jobs wherever I went, wherever he went.

Although Pam feels lucky to have found work, she feels frustration as well.

The moving has been very frustrating to me because I haven't been able to pursue any type of career advancement. I've more or less stayed in a stagnant state. Having children, if we were in one community, I could still build within the school system or within the community, whereas the moving has kept me parallel rather than going up the ladder, which I haven't enjoyed. But that's been more due to my husband's job changes than to having children, I think. I've thought about it a lot, and I don't think that I would be happier were I single and building. It might be about the same. I think I would have probably reached some level of frustration anyway, and this just puts it off to an older age.

Before having a child, Pam and Marty enjoyed a close and active relationship.

It was like we weren't married — but that obviously implies certain prejudices as far as I'm concerned. I would say it was like an affair as opposed to being married. We both worked, we both came and went as we pleased, and made love when we pleased, and ate when we pleased. There wasn't a need for structure. And we did almost everything together — a lot of sports, which has been very difficult since we had Sarah. We did a lot of ski touring and backpacking, things that you just can't do with young children.

At the time of the interviews, Pam and Marty were both thirty-four, their daughter was almost five, and they were expecting twins to be born in the next couple of weeks. Pam was a mother and homemaker, Marty a college professor. They owned the modest home in which they lived.

Pam and Marty had been married three years when they decided to have a baby. Neither of them felt emotionally committed to becoming parents.

We started talking about whether or not we wanted to have children, and decided if we did we really should do something about it. My parents had been a lot older, and I really didn't want to do that. I didn't mind taking time out. I felt that I would very much like to have a child and see what it was like. I have always liked to have all the experiences one can in life, and it seemed a shame to pass that by. And he agreed. It was more of an academic decision than you would think it would be. It wasn't a great emotional craving on either of our parts.

It was sort of, "Do you want a kid?" "Yeah, we should probably try that."

I think that we both felt we would be missing out on something that could be neat. But, you know, we probably equated it more with ski touring than we did with anything. We went into adulthood having to learn to ski, but what joy we've gotten out of that. Most things that we have tried, that we hadn't experienced that other people had said were good, seemed to have redeeming virtues. We both thought that it would be something we really would want to do.

Compared to some of our friends, I don't think that we were very emotional about it. I mean we have both been very pleasantly surprised. We both enjoy Sarah very much, and we were surprised, I would say, after she was born and now, that we have gotten as much pleasure out of it as we have. We sort of felt it to be something that we wouldn't want to pass by, and that we would regret, but we also didn't like what we were giving up. If we had known everything we were giving up, we probably wouldn't have done it. The first year or so of her life was really shocking — how much your life changes, how much freedom in fact one does give up.

At age twenty-eight, Pam went off the pill in order to become pregnant.

The pregnancy was uneventful and fantastic. I was probably more emotional, but that's all. Several people commented on the fact that there were no problems; they were amazed that I appeared happy. We were really lucky it was a well-thought-out decision, and we weren't eighteen or twenty-one, we were twenty-eight, twenty-nine. It was something that we both felt anxious about because the more pregnant you get, the more the enormity of what you've done and that you can't go backwards is upon you. But we were both very positive.

Pam worked until she was eight months pregnant with Sarah. Then she stopped. Her plan was to take time out from her career to give her child a good start.

I thought more and more about the fact that although I could influence people teaching, there was this greater potential to influence a child as far as the world of tomorrow. I had never liked infants; I looked forward more to a child of an older age than an infant. Neither of us is very religious, so that if there was a part of us that was going to live after us this child would be it.

Marty didn't care whether I stayed at home or whether I employed someone and went to work. But I cared. I felt that if I was going to have a child I would like to do the majority of the preschool education. Just because it's brainwashing; they absorb so much during that time. I wanted to do my brainwashing on my own child rather than have someone else do it, so that it had some chance of having an outlook that was morally compatible with ours.

When she decided to stay home to mother full time, part of Pam's plan was to space her two children closely together. That did not work out.

This pregnancy was thought out too, and a decision was made about it. We took somewhat longer to conceive than we did with Sarah, so there is a bit more space than intended. We were off by a year and a half. Our lives have been so haywire the last two years that it's probably just as well, but it has spread out my early childhood years a bit more than I had anticipated. I had said that if I wasn't pregnant by September I wasn't going to get pregnant, because I didn't feel that I could have a bigger space. They [the twins] just barely squeezed in there.

Pam plans to stay home with the twins.

I feel about them the way I felt about Sarah. If they drive me crazy, then I'll go back to work, because it's one thing to stay home when you're doing good things and it's something else to just stay home and scream and yell and be a bitchy mother. If I'm compatible with them, which I was lucky to be with Sarah, then I will stay home and work part time. If, on the other hand, I find that I can't handle it emotionally and I'm driving the family crazy, then I'll go to work and get someone who can give them the type of support that I think they should get.

Although Pam planned both of her pregnancies and in each case was pleased to be having her children, she is rather negative about the experience of pregnancy.

There's not much I like about being pregnant. I don't find it as negative an experience as a lot of women do because my body's fairly strong, but generally I don't find it positive or negative. I mean if I could have a child by keeping myself in a different way, I would certainly do it — cut off my big toe or something.

I don't like the responsibility. If you have a headache, you can't take aspirin, you take Tylenol. And you shouldn't smoke, and you shouldn't drink, and you should get sleep, and you drink milk until it comes out your ears. No, you shouldn't eat a doughnut, you should have a cheese sandwich instead. Or not going horsebackriding and skiing — the physical limitations.

Her feelings are intensified by her current pregnancy with the twins, which is more difficult than was her first pregnancy.

I did not feel at all frightened with Sarah. Nothing went wrong throughout the pregnancy with Sarah. It just seemed a totally natural process. I realize twins are probably natural, too, but I've always felt that this is an unnatural pregnancy. I'll be glad when it's over with.

During Pam's first pregnancy, she and Marty took Lamaze classes together. She delivered Sarah by natural childbirth and went home twenty-four hours later. Their geographical distance from kin meant they had no outside help when she got home, but Marty pitched in.

Being on the opposite coast from our families — if we had been on the same coast we might have felt more free to ask for help. When you get offers that someone will come and help you but it's going to cost them six hundred dollars round trip, and they have their own problems, you aren't quite so free to say, "Yes, we'd love to have you."

Marty was my help. We were much greater martyrs in our younger days than we are now. I don't know if I would do that again, but we were sure we could do it all quite adequately by ourselves. He was around all the time. We only lived half a mile from his school. He probably did something like fix breakfast, then go in and work for a couple of hours, come home and fix lunch, and go back for a couple of hours.

With the twins, we are going to have as much help as possible. Marty's mother is going to come as soon as we tell her to. She'll probably not be able to stay too long because her mother lives with them. Also, two ladies who are in their fifties, one of them has babysat for Sarah, agreed to assist us. I have talked with them and plan to employ them part time, as much as needed (that we can afford).

Pam's plan for help with the twins reflects memories of the postpartum period after Sarah was born.

I'm sure it appeared at times to be quite overwhelming; yet, on the opposite side, she was so much more fascinating than I expected. I was nursing her and all these things, and I'm sure everything physically was going together to make me like this child more. Even now, since I had Sarah, I look at other people's infants and it's just an infant. And when I look at pictures of Sarah as an infant, she was just an infant. But Marty and I thought that she was really beautiful and that she was delightful and all these things, although I got very tired and she awoke every couple of hours and things like that. But we did a lot; we probably did too much. We were sure that we weren't going to have our lifestyle changed. So, as a result, I'd get up every two hours and nurse her, we went to parties and took her with us, and we went camping with her for six weeks when she was five weeks old. We both enjoyed her, although it was certainly shocking to find out I couldn't just walk to the store when I wanted to.

I think we were both tired and bitchy; it wasn't a stage that we would care to go back to. We've talked about it some as far as this pregnancy; having been through the other one, we're aware of the fact that we will probably be tired and bitchy. We're less defensive than we were then and, hopefully, can handle it. I certainly went through a stage of trying to be a perfect mom and all these things I'd never been before, but that I felt this need to be. And he did also. He got this nervous disorder.

This time we are going to employ people as much as possible. We'll go out and leave the baby. We never left Sarah with a sitter until she was eleven months old. We were sure that she would just die instantly if anyone else cared for her. Whereas, I'm sure that the twins will be fine if I go out. Probably they will never be quite as secure as Sarah if it requires as much support as Sarah got. I thought that she was marvelous and extended myself. I would never put her down to let her cry after I had tried everything else. I would just sit there for hours and rock her, or let her suck on me when I had no milk, if I thought she needed that. Whereas, I'm just sure that with two you can't do that. So they'll just be raised differently.

Pam breastfed Sarah for about a year.

I enjoyed it until about ten months and then I got tired of it. I started to wean her, but I wasn't very successful. I finally just stopped. We had been to the zoo with Marty in San Diego, and we were coming back to Los Angeles, and I remember very specifically she was not hungry but she was crabby because she was tired and she wanted to nurse. Marty was tired, and I wasn't tired so I was driving. And she just wouldn't have anything to do with Marty because she wanted to nurse. And I just felt that it had gone on long enough, that our relationship had to get back into a normal family, which means you take care of daddy and the kid fits in, as opposed to stopping and having daddy drive when he's tired, so I could nurse this little thing that's old enough not to need this.

Pam loved how connected she felt to Sarah.

I never had anything that was a part of me, since I was adopted. I found that to be very special. And I had never been needed, certainly not with the intense need that an infant feels for you. I wouldn't have said before I had her, even now it sounds strange, but I do remember that as being a neat feeling: that you really were important or that you could do something better than anyone else.[1]

In fact, Pam enjoyed infant care far more than she expected, but she did not love it.

> It was more fun than I thought it would be, but it isn't one of the greater joys of mine. I took Sarah to swimming lessons when she was six months old mainly because I couldn't figure out what you were supposed to do. Here I was at home with this infant, and I was supposed to be doing all these wonderful things. She wasn't doing things fast enough for me. I look back, and she's always done things very quickly, which we are lucky about, but I got very bored so I started inventing these things for us to do for a while.

In spite of her willingness to stop working, the boredom of infant care led her back to teaching, very part time, when Sarah was one.

> After she was born I didn't teach for a year, but my husband felt that I was bordering on insanity, so he strongly suggested that I do something. I met a lady in the park who was teaching English as a Second Language at an adult school nearby, two nights a week. Her husband had just accepted a new job, so she was giving up the position. I went and interviewed for it and got it. So I started teaching two nights a week.

Pam continued teaching ESL into her current pregnancy and plans to resume the semester after the twins are born.

When Sarah was an infant, Pam was home as her primary caretaker, but Marty was very involved with family responsibilities as well.

> I nursed. He was up at night when the kid was screaming, but mainly he did all the cooking and housecleaning, the grocery shopping, all the peripheral things that he could do, until she slept through the night and I was able to relieve him of some of that. I wanted to relieve him mainly because I tend to be physically stronger than he is. Whenever he does too much he gets sick.

I did more childcare. He would certainly change her if he was holding her and she was wet or messy. He never called me to change her. He certainly handled her and played with her every day, although I would say until the last year he probably didn't enjoy her as much as I did. She became verbal quite early, which was very helpful for her. He did everything, and he did it fairly regularly, except that it didn't always work out well. So that an awful lot of times when she would fall asleep he would say to me, "Why don't you get out of here and do something and if she wakes up I'll take care of her," as opposed to taking her when she was awake and going someplace. Because he knew within twenty minutes she would start crying, and he couldn't do anything about it. So actually he would kick me out and keep her there so if she started screaming he wouldn't be in the middle of a store.

I think things are really different now. Marty, for one, is already doing all the grocery shopping and has been as I became more pregnant. And he does most of the laundry, and he does a lot more things around the house than he used to. He's much more sensitive to doing it, when he sees something that needs to be done, than when we first got married. I mean he just didn't see them.

The sharing of household responsibilities has changed several times in their marriage. Before they had a child there was a lot less to do. They tended to let things go and then do what was pressing together. With a newborn, much more needed to be done. During postpartum Marty did most of the household tasks, but when Pam was back on her feet she took on those responsibilities in addition to childcare. When that began to overwhelm her, Marty began to help more. He helps more with household responsibilities now than earlier in their marriage, especially during her pregnancy. They still have a casual approach to housecleaning, but Marty helps with the things that they feel require attention.

I do almost all the cooking. He does most of the dishwashing. The housecleaning doesn't get done very often. I washed the floors when we moved here six months ago. They haven't been touched since then, except for being swept, till about a month ago when Marty and I were thinking about putting down a new floor, and I thought I really should get this cleaned before someone comes in or they're just going to be grossed out. The lady across the street doesn't have much money and has offered several times to do things for money. So I had her come over and do them. Then they looked so nice — Marty and I were so amazed that we decided not to put down a new floor. What I mean is we are extremely lazy. Marty probably picks up more than I do. I probably dust and vacuum more that he does.

Pam still does most of the childcare, but Marty has become more involved over the past year.

Until about December I put her to bed much more. But when my mother was ill and I was out of town Sarah discovered that Daddy was much more competent than she ever thought he was. And ever since that period when they were here together for several weeks, she often requests him and he does bedtime as much, if not more, than I do now. They went to see "Star Wars" and the Peabody Museum. They've climbed up Sleeping Giant a few times. He took her for a walk — this weekend they went out and walked up to the grocery store. All these things have changed a lot. They seemed to like each other but to be in awe of each other for a long time. That is not true now, which is great.

The family lives on Marty's salary of about thirty-one thousand dollars a year. In fact, planning for breaks in Pam's employment, they've always lived on Marty's salary. This saved them the trauma of decreasing their standard of living when Pam stopped working and also provided a nest egg.

We never lived on both our salaries; we saved mine. So we had built up a fairly good cushion. In fact, it was quite large until we put it into the downpayment of the house.

They live frugally.

We try not to charge anything. We try to pay cash for whatever we're buying. When we don't have enough money in the bank account, we don't buy it. When I see something that I want to buy for myself, if it's cheap I buy it, if it's not I don't. I would never go and spend hundreds of dollars without Marty, but I would certainly, in the course of a normal month, buy whatever I wanted to.

They put fifty or a hundred dollars from Marty's earnings into savings every month. Pam is not sure of the exact amount because Marty takes care of the finances.

Marty pays the bills most of the time but he looks forward to the day that I will. I would love to. I would love to have little charts around where I knew what went out a year and where it went to and everything. I have these great designs — ledgers and things everybody gets in school. When our house is big enough that I could have as much of a workspace area as he does for files and things, I could compete with him along those lines. I did it before we were married, and I find that it sometimes causes him anxiety and it doesn't cause me anxiety, so I would just as soon do it. He really hates to do it, whereas I think it's great fun.

They do not aspire to a higher standard of living, yet there are some extras they would like.

Marty and I talked about what we would do with more money. We would have to be very careful not to have it disappear. You could eat steak more often or have a little bit better quality car— there's all sorts of small things that one could do that you wouldn't even know where it went. But we would attempt not to do that but stay on the same standard of living that we have and take more trips and hire more babysitters.

If she had not had children, Pam knows she would still be working.

I'd be working and I would be, hopefully, administering a Title I for the State of Connecticut — or at least participating in that, doing half teaching and half administrating. Title I is remedial reading, Title VIII is library funds for inner-city kids and things like that. Most of the work I've done has been in remedial reading and English as a Second Language, on a secondary level with inner-city kids.

Her expectations for fifteen or twenty years in the future, when her kids will be teens, are that she will be working. She has several interests that she hopes to pursue.

If we ever live in one community long enough, I would very much like to do something slightly political and get on a school board or something like that. I would enjoy also working as, but not solely as, a classroom teacher. I have seven years experience and also have some definite views on how I think things can be run better. I'd enjoy trying some of them out.

In fact, Pam expects to go back to work as soon as the twins are in school.

I will probably go back to classroom teaching for a while and then, if we were in the community for long enough, I would explore opportunities of what else I might do. I definitely cannot envision myself being at home without children. I mean I don't like housework very much. And I don't like women's groups and volunteer groups very much. At the least I might go back to school for a while to get my thoughts up to date, then get back to full-time work. Unless we were so affluent that I could just travel, then I'd leave Marty and the kids — that's not really true. No, if we had more money, we might leave the kids and travel together. I wouldn't really find it particularly enjoyable to go alone. But I wouldn't mind having a job within the state that required traveling within the state.

Perhaps because she recently lost her own mother, perhaps because she has a self-reflective nature, Pam is very analytical about her own mothering style. She feels her mother served as a strong model of female independence and resourcefulness, but that her mother was a different type of mother.

> I was raised with less encouragement to touch and feel, and perhaps break, in the process of experimenting. And I was raised primarily in a house and not actively encouraged to be with children until after school age. I rarely had children in the house who were my friends. I was encouraged to go outside and play, which is good, but I was not particularly encouraged to want to do things like cook with mother or something like that. Generally speaking, I was criticized, well not criticized but I was told to go out in the backyard and play or go someplace else and play, and I didn't do a lot of things together with my mother. I wasn't raised with an attitude of, "Hey, that's good." I do think that's good. I try to be supportive of Sarah. My mother's philosophy was that if you told a kid that they were good too much you would make them conceited and they'd be hard to live with. And, in fact, she was worried about what's going to happen to Sarah because we tell her she's good a lot.

Pam used to feel she was a lenient parent, but is reevaluating that assessment now that Sarah is in nursery school three mornings a week.

> I thought I was less strict than most other people I knew, but I find that, Sarah's teacher claims, that she is very mature and responsible. I'm not sure whether I have been more strict than I intended to be or whether, just by virtue of the fact that we've moved around a lot, we've constantly had to redefine and set up rules and re-teach them and things like this. Also, since we got some of mother's furniture, there's been a bit more rules about certain things than there were before, just because when she was younger there was nothing that possibly could be broken, and I didn't really enforce anything as far as jumping on sofas and beds. She has responded well. If you ask her not to do something, generally she won't do it. I guess I'm in a middle place now. There are some parents that I feel when I talk to them, "Well, why don't you tell him not to do that." So I guess I'm not as lenient as I thought I was.

She sees herself as different from most of the women she knows. She is committed to her career and looks forward to returning to full-time work, which remains an important aspect of her identity. Yet, she is a devoted mother and feels very committed to being with her preschool children. She feels less conventional than the mothers around her, although more conventional than she ever expected she would be.

Around here everybody seems to go to church, and we don't. I think it's important that I talk to Sarah about the wonders of nature and talk to her about God, but I don't feel church attendance is as crucial as most people I meet in New England do. I've gained a lot more acceptance than I had when she was younger for not raising her strangely, a lot more feeling that middle-class type environments and goals were good things to expose her to, as opposed to always making her different.

As far as running the house, I probably enjoy being with her much more than most other parents of children her age. The other day the mother of a child in her nursery school and I were talking, and she was saying that she had been home with her daughter on Tuesday all day for the first time in a long time — she's more affluent than we are and often hires someone to stay with her—and that she just went crazy and that the child wouldn't play by herself and wouldn't leave her alone and she just couldn't stand that. She felt that the child really needed nursery school. She couldn't stand being around her all day. Although she basically likes the child, she just couldn't think of what to do with her all day.

Most of the people that we've been forced to meet, especially Sarah and I, whether we wanted to or not, are mothers of preschool children and neighbors. The majority are our age or younger, probably. A lot of them are Catholics and have more than one child and find it strange that I don't look forward to infanthood and that I want to go back to work. They're much more traditional than my views — though not than my role at the moment.

People here seem to have families that are larger. They tend not to live as far from their relatives and they tend to socialize a lot more with their families than I'm accustomed to.

I feel glad we have some friends that live very different lives than we do. At times I think about them as to whether or not they're being exploited — some that are working that I know don't want to work. We have one couple that are good friends: the woman was going to work for a while until her husband got a real physics job, but unfortunately he is unemployed so she is supporting them, which is fine. Except he is always going into the mountains for a month or something like that. He goes on a lot of trips with Marty. They're several years older than we are, and I know she very much wanted to have children before she was forty.

As a young woman, Pam was an independent thinker critical of traditional marriage and motherhood. In her mid-thirties she still perceives herself as holding unconventional attitudes; she does not see herself as much of a housekeeper and considers herself a good mother in spite of her mixed feelings about infancy and her eagerness to return to her career. At the same time, she knows her role as mother/homemaker is more conventional than her attitudes and looks forward to the future when it will take less of her time. All this makes her feel "different" from her friends and neighbors, yet satisfied with her choices.

Pam has a positive self-image as a mother and feels she has gained a lot from motherhood. She feels that having a child has made her a more understanding person.

I was teaching remedial reading and I was sure that I could change the world. And after Sarah was born it was just so obvious from all the little infants her age that I knew that they couldn't so easily be changed. Watching them develop and knowing their mothers and knowing essentially how they were raised, it was so obvious that there was so much more to heredity involved than I had ever wanted to believe. I don't know if it's heredity, but I mean that it seems like the child was just born more crabby or less secure — temperament. I mean you could work on degrees of it but you couldn't change the totality. I can't believe it's all parents. I don't believe that I've been a better parent than a lot of my friends. Yet I see Sarah achieving more and thinking more positively of herself than some of her peers that I think have been raised just as appreciated, and I just think that she was born sort of smiling and self-confident. At least I feel she was.

Pam feels that having a child has also affected her emotionally, in very deep and positive ways.

It has made me know myself much better. It has made me more organized, more tolerant. It's shown me both the breadth to which I can extend and also the limitations that I have that weren't really tested before. I guess emotionally, especially, I didn't fully appreciate, although I thought I did when I got married, the depth of caring for someone else. The feelings one has in high school, live or die with some boyfriend or something, sort of passed as one became more mature. And I certainly have very strong feeling towards my husband. But that type of almost instinctive passionate-type caring, where you become so frightened that something will happen to them; that's sort of scary at times. In fact, that's one reason we decided to have another child. I really wasn't sure if I could emotionally survive something that would be very tragic. So we sort of thought if we spread it out a little bit we'd have a better chance of making it sane to old age.

Pam never imagined she would be a wife/homemaker/mother. As a young woman she was critical of that traditional path and oriented towards a career instead. She has not given up her career-oriented self-image, nor adopted a stereotypically traditional homemaker one. Yet, she has chosen at different junctures to marry, to have children, and to stay home as primary caretaker. Because she has a good education, career experience, and a supportive husband, as well as an organized and self-conscious approach to her choices, she feels in control of her life and able to change her mind and return to full-time employment whenever she is ready. She knows she has gained a lot from her role as mother and feels successful at it. Although she suffers some frustration due to her lack of career advancement, she is happy with her choice to take time off to start her family.

7

Ellen

I thought it would be the greatest thing to stay home.

Ellen, like Linda, simply expected to marry and raise a family. She went to junior college to learn secretarial skills so that she would have "something to fall back on," but she never considered preparing for a career. In spite of the problems she saw in her parents' marriage, she had a romantic view of what marriage and motherhood would be like.

She worked many years before her first baby came along. She started selling fabrics part time at the age of sixteen, as soon as she was old enough to get working papers. Again like Linda, she wanted money to buy things for herself. She worked in retail sales throughout high school and college. After college, she held a secretarial position for more than six years, until her first child was due. She was glad to leave work; she expected to love staying home with her baby. Six months later she changed her mind.

Ellen was a woman without career aspirations; she just expected to be a full-time mother and homemaker. Yet, she quickly found that she missed the sociability and feeling of accomplishment that work provided her. She returned to part-time sales, then took in office work, then returned to sales. She remains primarily a mother and homemaker; she fits her work hours into evenings and weekends, when her husband is typically home. Ellen is one of four of the thirty women who has no career commitment, planned to be home full time, but instead is employed.

Since Ellen's goal was to be a wife and mother, at first she and Bud did little in the way of family planning. Her marriage changed drastically, however, once there was a baby. Being a mother was different than she expected it to be. With the child came friction, much less doing things together, and financial tension because she no longer had her salary. These changes caused Ellen to develop a strategy. She returned to work part time to earn some spending money. Her employment gave her husband some quality time with the children and her a sense that she was different from her friends, but it did not restore the old conjugal order.

In fifteen years Ellen plans to be working. She is preparing to get a realtor's license because she likes houses and likes flexible hours. Although caring for two small children is stressful, she cannot imagine life without them.

🐛 🐛 🐛

I always admired nurses, but because I get very wheezy at the sight of blood I knew that was not for me. Back when I was interested in doing something, it was going to college, yes, but it was going to college to do something that I'd be able to fall back on. There was never any talk of becoming a lawyer, or a doctor, or anything like that. It was just assumed that someday I would marry, and so I assumed it, too. So that kind of drive girls seem to have today wasn't really present in any of the girls that I knew. Although one did go on to be a doctor, that wasn't typical talk.

I wanted to get married. I did think that it would be a lot more romantic than it is, but I had no Hollywood fantasies that we'd live happily ever after. I do feel, though, that I didn't have any idea what went into being a mother. I was not at all realistic. Things have happened even recently that Dr. Spock never wrote about, that I had never thought I'd have to deal with.

Ellen grew up in a family of five: her parents, herself, and two younger brothers. Both her parents had high school diplomas; her mother had also attended secretarial school. Her father worked his way up in General Electric, relocating his family three times when he moved with the company. He retired as a manager. Her mother, who had worked before she married, returned to work as a secretary when Ellen was a teenager. The family was aspiring to be middle class, which required a good deal of stretching financially.

It was a struggle, as it is today, to have a nice home and nice things. That's a struggle. It was most difficult to keep going and move each time. Each time you buy a new home they go up in price, and the moving expenses, and all those kinds of things. And then, of course, when we were here I was getting into my teens, and they were thinking about sending me to school, and, at that point, where I went was not inexpensive. So all these things contributed, and then, of course, the two boys coming up — so it's never been an easy street.

In fact, Ellen remembers a lot of tension between her parents about money.

On the whole, they disagreed about money more than anything. It would be a disagreement about should we have lessons, dancing lessons. My father wasn't against us doing it, but we couldn't afford it, that kind of thing. That was a big bone of contention at home.

When I was a child, from the time we came here when I was maybe eight, this was when I really got involved meeting lots of people, lots of kids, and seeing their parents. Only being naturally exposed to the other people could I actually make a judgement, and I would say my parents didn't get along that well. In the back of my mind, I realized that their marriage was not the loving, affectionate marriage that I would have liked to have seen.

My father had a lack of knowledge about how to be affectionate, how to be loving. I think that some men feel that because they are living at home, and because they have married, and because you have children, and because they bring home the money, that means they love you. I'm sure they do, but there is also another part of it that has to be present which is outward affection, which some men find very difficult.

I can remember one of my mother's biggest complaints was she would drive up with a car full of groceries, and he would be sitting there, and unless she asked he wouldn't help her with them — things like that. That's one thing I've learned from my mother: if you want something done you'd better ask, and I ask. I don't sit around and stew because it wasn't done; I ask.

Nonetheless, Ellen remembers having had a very happy childhood.

It was all a lot of fun, particularly back in New Jersey. We had a playground right nearby, and we used to go during the summer. They used to have all kinds of fun things to do up there — make those wire flowers and have plastic over them and oh, the lariat. Is that what they called them? You weave them out of the plastic pieces. Lots of stuff like that. And then we moved to Syracuse. I had a girlfriend who had a horse. We had a big hill, and we would ride up bareback on the horse. There was a big gully, and we'd go down there and pick up quartz out of the side of it, and then we just dreamed down there. It was just pleasant and quiet. And then when we came here we used to play hide and seek and swim in the pond nearby and ride horses. I did have a nice childhood as far as I can remember, very enjoyable. The only drawback to the whole thing was that my mother and I did not get along very well. We would fight quite often. It bothered me. I didn't like it, but I have very strong opinions, and she has very strong opinions. I guess that's typical with girls.

Although Ellen never dreamed of a career, she started working when she was quite young.

I started babysitting when I was in my early teens, and when I could actually work and hold down a job I was sixteen years old. A girlfriend and I opened a clothes fabric department in Bradlees, and we worked there in fabrics because she sewed beautifully and I sewed some. From there I went to another department store and worked through the last few high school years, through college. I tried to hold down a night job there while I worked full time as a secretary in New Haven, but found that wasn't very good at all. I just couldn't, got too run down, got sick. So I just cut that out; I worked only full time at my secretarial job. I worked as a secretary for six and a half years.

Mainly I worked because I wanted things; particularly at that age I wanted clothing, of course, and that was one way of doing it. I guess a lot of babysitting money went towards learning to drive. My father was dead set against me getting my license and refused to pay. At that time, you took it from a driving school, and so I earned enough money to take that course and did that. I can't say that I gave my family any money to help them. It was mainly so I could buy my clothing. I probably didn't need all that I wanted either.

Ellen and her husband attended the same high school, at the same time, but did not meet until they both were in college. She commuted to a nearby junior college; he attended a local four-year college.

We went to high school together, but I was dating the hockey goalie, and he was a football player. It was a rather large class, and so we really didn't know one another then. I was still dating the hockey goalie through college, and then we kind of let things go, and I was having a New Year's Eve party, and a girlfriend had suggested that we might need a couple more guys, and she knew a couple to call. And one of the boys that she called was Bud. I don't know why, but we kind of struck up a relationship at that New Year's Eve party, and then I guess a few weeks later he called me for a date.

They eased into a relationship, dating steadily but not heavily.

I was always the type of person who didn't sit around waiting for the telephone to ring because I had lots of boyfriends. When I say boyfriends, I mean friends. We had a wonderful group, and we would go do things constantly. We weren't the typical high school kids that went to parties and made out. We didn't do those things. If we were at a party, at twelve at night we might go get our skates and go down to Clark's pond and go ice-skating and stuff. We just had a great time — some of the best years of my life were my last two years of high school. So I didn't sit around and wait. I guess we ended up, not too long after that, dating one another exclusively, but not heavily. We would date maybe on a Saturday evening, and he would go out with the guys on Friday. I talked to him maybe once or twice a week, stuff like that — probably for a good six or eight months. Then he finally started pulling away from the Friday nights and coming to see me.

Ellen and Bud dated for two and a half years before becoming engaged and got married a year after that.

Although their courtship was not passionate, Ellen remembers with pleasure their marital relationship before the kids were born.

> It was so nice because we could do things together. We'd come and go as we pleased, and there weren't the added strings. I'd get ready, he'd get ready, and we'd go. We were both working a lot to save money. We'd decide to do this, and we'd do it. We'd decide to buy this, and we'd buy it. We did most things together — vacation, whatever. Today it's, "You get him ready, and I'll get this one ready," and, "Well, then I don't have any time to get ready." And, "Gosh, do you have to take all that stuff?" "Well, I have to." It's a more constant friction.

At the time of the interview, Ellen and Bud were both thirty-four, and their two children were six and one. Bud was a banker, Ellen was a full-time homemaker and part-time salesperson, Seth attended afternoon kindergarten, and Emily was at home.

Ellen and Bud had been married three years when their first child came along.

> We didn't decide. I guess we were very lucky because we didn't use any birth control. We were careful. I didn't use birth control pills because I was frightened of them at the time. So we were lucky, and it just happened, and that was fine. We'd give up now and then, but we were careful. Rhythm didn't work very well with me and still doesn't because of my cycle. Withdrawal, things like that. It just happened; there was no planning about this at all. After Seth was born, then I went on

the birth control pill. I was on those for three years and that was when I turned thirty and decided that was enough of that. Then it was another year later that I got pregnant with Emily.

Ellen was happy to be pregnant the first time.

Happy and scared at the same time. The first time scared because you just don't know what's ahead, but thrilled. With Seth I breezed through it — no problem. The neat thing about being pregnant for me was the attention from family and friends. But, on the whole, I did not like being pregnant. I just felt so uncomfortable and so big and so clumsy.

Bud was with me through the whole thing when both of them were born. He was not as involved as some men get. We didn't take classes. I had girlfriends to talk to and stuff but, until you actually experience it, I don't think that anyone can tell you what it's like because it's so different for everyone anyway. I can recall the minute Seth was born I just sobbed and sobbed and sobbed uncontrollably. I didn't get sick like one of my girlfriends did. I just couldn't control myself. It was — I don't know what. I think it was excitement and relief. Things were all right, and it was a boy, and the whole thing.

Of course, I had been sitting around for six whole days. The contractions started ten minutes apart and continued like that for three days, down and up, so there was no sleep. They were not pains that you could sleep through. I finally got down to five minutes apart regularly. I would go to five minutes, but not regularly, until Wednesday at around two o'clock and we called, and the doctor said bring her down. So we went to his office, and he examined me and said, "Okay, we're going to admit you," and even at that point, after sitting around for three days, I said, "Really? Are you sure? I'm not sure I want to do this." It was a little late to decide! I was admitted to the hospital about 3:30, and he was born at 10:29.

He was born on Wednesday. Here we got into a little bit of a problem. I certainly would have come home on Saturday, but my husband was in a wedding and, of course, all the relatives, mother and father and everybody, were attending the wedding so who would have brought me home, or who would have stayed with me? So we just decided that it would probably be better to stay until Sunday. So Bud brought me home on Sunday and took off then for a week at Amherst College for a course, and my mother stayed with me.

Ellen feels that, although unplanned, the timing of her first child was good.

It was God's will, because we certainly didn't plan it. There is no good time to have children, but, if there was, that was the best, because we were in a financial position to be able to purchase a home. If we had had one earlier, we wouldn't have been able to do that, and if we had one later we might not have decided to have one at all, because once you get into the house, and eventually we had to get a new car, and we should have carpeting... so it just worked out.

Ellen's first labor and delivery was so long and painful that she decided one child would be enough.

After he was born, I said that was it. No more of this. Bud, at that point, said too, no more. But when Seth was about four, I guess, we started thinking, "Well, gee, it really would be nice to have another one." And it was much easier, I mean except for the four months of colic, which was brutal. The adjustment on my part, and I believe on Bud's part also, has not been as great, not nearly so great as when we had the first. Really, having Seth was the biggest adjustment.

She loved the idea of leaving work when Seth was born, but not the reality.

I thought it would be the greatest thing in the world to stay home. However, that lasted about six months. I really missed the contact with people. Particularly in this neighborhood, maybe not in others but this is an older neighborhood, and mostly everybody's out to work, and mostly all the kids are in school.

In fact, there were many unanticipated changes during Seth's infancy which contributed to Ellen's difficult postpartum adjustment.

My own little world, until six years ago, was very secure and happy. Six years ago my mother and father were divorced; Seth was just about six months old. The most traumatic thing that ever happened to me until six years ago was that we had had a dog for fifteen years, and he was a very tremendous part of our family, and he was killed, and I just fell to pieces. So that goes to show you the kind of life that I led. I felt very happy most of the time, I remember. I didn't make twirling. I guess that was another tremendous disappointment, but nothing as earthshaking as what's happened in the last six years. Everything was coming along just nice and smooth. A few bumps here and there, and then the whole thing fell apart.

I swore I'd never see my mother again. She was to blame. Well, I shouldn't say totally because it does take two always, but it was totally foreign to anything I had ever been taught or knew about. She had met someone else.

Of course, my mother and I really never did get along until I had my first child, and then we seemed to really find something in common. We are very different in a lot of ways, and we finally had something tremendously in common, and then six months later the whole thing fell apart. Then she did remarry.

I knew for a long time that they didn't get along, well before the divorce. I think I would have accepted it much better if it had been a mutual agreement that we just don't get along, instead of one going that way.

Besides having a newborn child, my first, I then had my father to take care of, to make sure he was okay, to make sure he didn't turn out to be a bum, to make sure he had a meal in him at least three times a week. I helped him with finding a new place to live, helped him sell the house that he had, helped him get rid of the furniture and buy new furniture. Then my mother remarried, and he was pretty well set, my dad. He's doing good. Then about a year and a half later my mother's husband died. I had been pregnant with my second child. We had finally come to a meeting of the minds. We had come to like her new husband. As a matter of fact, I helped them find their place that she now lives in. I was pregnant. I did not have a very good pregnancy with my daughter. He died about a month before I was due with her, and that was a tremendous shock. And then my husband was out of work a week after he died. And I was two weeks late in my pregnancy; I finally had to go in and be induced. I was very tired—I hadn't gotten much sleep since January. She was colicky, so I spent four months walking the floors and trying to keep track of my other one. The past six years have been a terrible, terrible, rude awakening to what life is really all about.

Although Ellen remembers difficulty adjusting to Seth's birth, especially in comparison to adjusting to Emily's arrival, Seth was the easier baby.

Seth was a wonderful baby. I didn't know it at the time —I just assumed that was what babies were like — but he was very, very good. He was on a four-hour schedule, and by the time he was eight weeks old he was sleeping through the night beautifully. He was very cute and smiley and it didn't take anything to get him to laugh. He was a very happy little baby. Emily is a different story. She was colicky, and it was a good solid four months before she started to come out of that. And that was difficult, particularly with having a five-year-old, also with the summer and having him out running around. I had to spend a lot of time with the baby just rocking her. And she is not nearly as friendly and outgoing as Seth. She's much more reserved and waits to see how she feels about things and people before she goes to them. Seth was different. He would go with anybody and still would.

I don't remember Seth crying at all, out of hunger or any-thing. Really, he was a very pleasant baby. He would wake up after four hours, and you would feed him and bathe him and play with him, and he was perfectly happy. He was seven pounds and half an ounce. He lost only a half an ounce in the hospital, and by the time we left he was right back up again. It was only several days that we were there. He came home at his birth weight and was taking a good four to six ounces. So he was a very good eater.

I could put him down for a nap or to bed without any trouble. When he was five months old he gave us trouble; he started screaming about going to bed. We let him scream, and after about two or three nights he realized that was the way it was going to be and didn't give us any trouble anymore. Emily, only since a week and a half, two weeks ago, has been fairly decent about going to bed. Emily has gotten better about it. From day one she would cry no matter what when you put her up for anything — nap, nighttime — and we let her cry. We let her cry two solid hours, and she's cried the whole time— she doesn't give up.

Although motherhood has been far more difficult than she anticipated, Ellen enjoys infant care.

I just like infants; my girlfriend doesn't like infants. She likes them when they get a bit older, mainly because she's frightened of them. I don't feel I was ever frightened. You worry about sickness and things like that. I do remember keeping them pretty close to me for a couple of months because of this crib death thing. I was very conscious of that, making sure that they were breathing. It doesn't bother me at all to change diapers or anything like that. Loss of sleep, that's the most difficult. With Seth, those first eight weeks seemed like an eternity, and with Emily it was an eternity. I wasn't sure I'd live through it.

Ellen's problems with Emily started during her pregnancy.

What I went through with her — I would not want to get pregnant again. Nothing comes easy to me. Everything seems to be much harder for me than everybody else. I just spent some very agonizing months. I don't know to this day what it is. During my pregnancy, from January until I gave birth to her on May 1st, something was not right. I couldn't walk very well, and I couldn't lie on either side. It was just agonizing pain, so I would not want to go through that again. Whatever it was, I spent from January until I had her sitting up on the couch trying to get some sleep at night.

Ellen tried to breastfeed Emily but did not succeed. She regrets not having breastfed Seth.

With Seth, it just didn't really enter my mind. With Emily, I tried solidly for a week and a half or so. I think if I had not breastfed her, if I had bottle-fed her, I would have known much sooner that there was something wrong, other than myself. I just thought there wasn't enough there, she wasn't getting enough — I just didn't know. It was terrible, and so I started then to supplement with the bottle and gradually weaning her from breastfeeding because I couldn't keep up with it. It was every half an hour, every hour, every hour and a half. I was just totally exhausted and, again, not knowing whether she was getting enough, whether she was hungry or what, until we realized that she was colicky and there was nothing else we could do about it.

I feel now, unfortunately, that the best time to do it is your first because you have nothing else to think about but the baby. That's all you have to concern yourself with. I'm sorry I didn't realize that at the time. With Emily, like I said, Seth was five years old, and I'm the type of mother who really likes to keep an eye on him, and when I have to run around outside looking for him and get nervous because I can't find him and have to deal with a colicky baby on top of it, it was very difficult. But my sister-in-law, she's doing it with her first and I think that's super. All she has to do is concentrate on that baby. That's what you have to do. You can't be nervous. You can't be thinking about other things. You just have to concentrate on that baby.

The day Bud brought Ellen and Seth home from the hospital he left to take a week-long course in Massachusetts. Ellen's mother stayed with her for the week and continued to help part time after that.

She stayed with me the whole week and then off and on for a few weeks after that. She would help me out with a couple of night feedings a couple of nights a week. She works, so she did take some time when I came home from the hospital. She is basically self-supporting, so she couldn't take too much. She would stop after work and help get dinner and walk with the baby, and sometimes she would stay over and let me get more night sleep.

After Emily was born, Ellen had less outside help. Her mother came again but left when her daughter-in-law needed help after the birth of her first child.

She spent kind of a week, but then my sister-in-law had her baby that next weekend, and my brother had to leave for summer camp, and she went and stayed down there for a week with my sister-in-law. This was difficult this time because Emily was colicky, and I also had Seth, and it was spring, and he was running all over creation. I was trying to keep track of him and take care of her. She took up a lot of time because we just had to watch her; there was nothing else we could do. My mother-in-law came over. She's older though. She would dust around and do things like that. She'd got very bad arthritis so that she really couldn't handle the baby too well.

Caring for newborn Seth was Ellen's responsibility. Bud was the breadwinner, Ellen the mother and homemaker. She did not consider it proper to ask Bud for help and turned, as may local women did, to her mother instead. This changed after colicky Emily was born five years later.

With Seth, Bud never got up and took a night feeding. I didn't feel that that was a proper thing to do as long as I could do it, and he had to get up and go to work, and I could rest during the day. But with Emily, after about two months solid of this, I finally just couldn't do it anymore, and I had to ask him if he would at least take every other night. And sometimes he would relieve me in feeding her baby food. As a matter of fact, he was the one who developed the system for getting food in her to begin with.

Ellen continues to be primarily responsible for home and child care, but she has managed to add part-time work to her schedule. Her part-time job requires childcare assistance which Bud usually provides. Her mother and mother-in-law serve as back-ups for when a meeting at work keeps him late.

Seth was born in June so not that first Christmas, but the Christmas after, I went back to sales and worked during Christmas. I did that off and on until about four years later. Then I took in some typing, and then I got on with my pregnancy with Emily. I guess about a month before she was born I stopped that because it was very hectic. I worked for one guy, and he was in and out all hours of the day and night with things to do, basically not very organized. He wanted me to keep it up afterwards, but I couldn't.

Now I work six to nine, but I can't tell you Monday, Wednesday, and Friday. It's just whenever they put me on the schedule. This past week I was working every night because they had a sale. But then there are times when I'll only work a couple of nights. Since January, every Monday night I've been taking a course in real estate, which I just finished up with the highest mark in the class. I've been contemplating going up to Hartford and taking the state exam. I like to keep busy. Housework is not my passion — I like to vacuum but not as a career. I like people, so I like to get out and meet people.

My husband comes home, and I have dinner ready, and he and Seth eat. Emily is usually fed. Sometimes we're able to eat together. If he's home by five-thirty or so, I'm able to eat with them, and then I take off from here close to ten of six if I can. Then he cleans up and takes care of things and puts them away.

I think it's been very good for him also because he is into the kids. He knows them well. Much different than in my parents' generation, when women going out to work was very rare so the fathers didn't get all that involved, particularly with babies. They didn't seem to, at least from what I saw. The mother took care of them; that was her job. I think it's changed a little bit here. It's good for him in that way, and it's not that long that he spends with them, an hour and a half tops, and for me I feel like I've accomplished something.

The help with the children that Bud provides is a big change in the marital division of labor and one that Ellen greatly appreciates. It has come about because of her desire to have a part-time job and as a result of her fighting with Bud about weekend time.

We used to have arguments about Bud playing golf. When we moved in here — we had Seth several months later — this whole house needed to be painted. Every weekend that he could he painted the house, and when he wasn't painting the house he was playing golf. I was, guess what, stuck home without any time, and I don't think he really understood that. An awful lot of men don't understand that women don't get a vacation and don't get weekends. One day just melts into

another. This was very difficult. This was a very large adjustment. It's only been in the last couple of years that the adjustment has been made.

I don't mind him playing golf at all. I think it's grand. It's
something that he enjoys doing, but I also enjoy doing things
and would like some time to do them too. So, if he's going to
play golf which is a rather lengthy sport, he gets up at five-
thirty, and he's out by six. Therefore, he's home by ten, ten-
thirty, eleven, and I'm able to perhaps take a couple of hours
in the afternoon for myself if I want to do something. It's
worked out much better than screaming and hollering because
he's gone ten to four. And that's the way it is when they play
every weekend if they don't get out early.

Ellen likes to work because it gives her a sense of accomplishment, gives her social contact, and gives her money of her
own.

It's really hard; I have very little to do with the money
situation. I would say he makes probably around thirty-two
or thirty-three thousand, somewhere around there. I do what
I need; he pays all the bills. I would consult him first on
something like buying clothes for myself; things today are so
expensive. I would consult him on that, but I'm not frivolous,
so he doesn't worry about that. We spend a lot of money, but
not on our backs and not on the house. It just goes. I don't
know where it goes. I just said the other day, I work mostly for
buying gifts. Actually, if you boiled it down, I probably do
work mostly for buying gifts, particularly all the money that I
make at Christmas. It has been this way for many years now.
I purchase all the Christmas gifts with the money that I make.
With the money I make, I have been able to buy new kitchen
curtains, a new bedspread.

I keep my money separate. If I put it in the checking account
it disappears. Right now I have a couple of checks right here
that I haven't cashed, because if I cash them they disappear.
Saturday I spent fifty dollars of my money, and it went for the
baby: vitamins and my son takes iron because he's borderline
anemic. Just crazy things. On occasion I'll need milk or something like that, and if I have it in my wallet I'll get it. But most
of the time that comes out of the checkbook.

Ellen, like most of the local women, had help from her extended family when her children were born and continues to depend upon kin for childcare assistance and for social life.

> We left Seth and went out together. My mother-in-law or mother would babysit, or my sister-in-law, and we would go places and do different things — not a lot — certainly not more than once a month. But neither of us like that. We are very homebody people, and when we do go we really enjoy it. But with Emily, the past year had not been a good one, so we didn't get out probably as much as we should have.
> We didn't take her out anywhere until she was more than three months old. That's how bad she was. I really couldn't take her anywhere. We usually go over to my mother-in-law's on Saturday evenings and have dinner, which I thoroughly enjoy. It sounds crazy, but I do enjoy it. And I would not go. I would rather stay home than inflict her screaming and crying on them.

Ellen feels close to both her family and Bud's. Their relatives are their friends. In addition to her mother and mother-in-law, they regularly see Ellen's father and her three sisters-in-law and their families.

> You can come here almost any night of the week and one of my family, or good friends, will be here for dinner or lunch or breakfast.

Her family is very important to her. When talking about what she would do if they had a bit more money, Ellen has lots of wants but she is quick to point out that family comes first for her.

> I would do a lot of things if we had more money. There are so many things that have to be done — mainly I would do things in my house. We need a new cellar door. We need all kinds of fixing things. I would love to have a picnic table. We contemplated buying a gas grill. Just little things. I've always said to my husband, too, money, I'd like to have it, no question about it, but money does not mean that much to me. For

instance, if he were to be offered a ten thousand dollar increase in pay in order to move to Texas, that would have no meaning for me at all. I wouldn't go to Texas for ten thousand dollars; I would stay here with my family.

Ellen sees her parenting style as very similar to that of her mother but is surprised by how hard it is to be a mother, how difficult it is to control her children, how different kids seem from what she remembers from her childhood.

I would say I am probably bringing them up the same way I was brought up, but they are so different from what I remember and what I'm told about when I was younger. I think you could ask almost anybody, and they will tell you that kids today are so different. I don't know what it is. They are not respectful. I still, to this day, will call somebody Mr. and Mrs. until I am told otherwise, and even then it kind of grates on me a little bit. But they are mouthy, they are fresh, and I can't see that I'm doing anything any different.

They are much harder to control than I thought they would be, unbelievably so. Really. My husband always says you don't want to break his [Seth's] spirit. No way I'd ever break that kid's spirit. I'd hate for him to be, "Yes, mommy, what would you like?" I wouldn't want him to be like that, but I sure wish he'd listen more, and when he listens I wish he'd do what he's heard. He's very, very hard to control, and I really don't know what it is.

Ellen plans not to have any more children. Since she and Bud are not using contraception, she has considered how she would handle an unwanted pregnancy.

I've thought about it. No question about it — I have thought about it. Right now what would be in my mind is I would just go and have a D & C. My husband might support that kind of decision. I would certainly tell him about it, but I would do it even if he objected. It's what I go through, and it has nothing to do with sex or my love for him, I just don't think I could make it. Maybe I could, but my pregnancy with Emily was such an unbelievable pregnancy.

In spite of the fact that she is home most of the time, Ellen is a bit defensive about her commitment to her home and family because she spends some time away from them, at work. She considers herself both similar to and different from her friends in the way she runs her family.

> I think I probably do it much the same way as my friends, but I take a little more for myself because I need it. My best girlfriend needs it but doesn't take it for many reasons. I go out to work, and I think she might like to, but yet she can't get it together to do it for one reason or another. She is very much concerned about her house and stuff like that; I'm concerned about my house but I feel like I need more than the constant housekeeping.
>
> I like to have a nice home, and I like to have a neat home, and I love being with my kids. That's why I would never go back full time, because I feel that my responsibility is to my children. My work is very flexible for me: I can do it or I can't do it. It's not going to be terribly disastrous if I can't make it because Emily got sick or something; they will survive. But I really do feel a need to accomplish something, instead of vacuuming and five minutes later there are crumbs all over the floor again. That's kind of depressing to me. So if I can go over and put in a few hours and feel as though I've accomplished something, it makes me feel better.

Ellen has established some control over her life by getting help from Bud, by taking part-time jobs, and by developing a personal plan for fertility control. None of these were part of her expectations for married life; she has changed and grown as a result of finding the reality of motherhood a lot harder than she anticipated. She also perceives that children and family life have changed since she was a child.

Ellen is already planning for the work she will do when her children are older.

> I like homes. I like to see homes and stuff like that. Maybe I'll be doing real estate, because I hope at that point to have my license. I'm going to take the state exam. The thing with

real estate is, I've now passed the course primarily to get to take the exam. Then I can take the exam, but then I can't get a license unless I have a job. So I have to have somebody promise me that they'll give me a job before I can get a license to do it. Maybe I'll run my own company or have my own company, but I don't think in terms of anything that could completely tie me up nine to five, except for a few weeks a year, again. That's not really living. I enjoy working, but I also would like to enjoy a lot more of the benefits of life then — especially fifteen years from now. I don't expect to be able to do them now, because with the kids and everything I'm not in the position to, but maybe fifteen years from now it would be a nice thing to do.

Though she looks forward to doing more and having more when her kids are grown, she does not regret having had children.

It seems like I've had them forever. I don't think I'd be very happy without them, because, as I said before, if I didn't have children probably it would be because I wanted more things or wanted to make more money, and I don't want to do those things. Someday perhaps, but I don't feel tied down.

Having children, it's had a tremendous impact, but an impact that you don't know about until it happens. It's just a natural course of living. For me, I couldn't imagine it any other way. I do have a girlfriend out in California who will not have children, and she's quite a jet setter. They go to the horse races, and she drives a Porsche. They go to Aspen, skiing, and then they go to the Bahamas for a holiday. I couldn't live that life! Sounds wonderful. She knows the movie stars like Meredith Baxter, and I think that's swell to hear about, but I couldn't live that life. I would be pressed to do that kind of thing. This is certainly stressful at times, but it's not a stressful living situation. I'm very comfortable with it. So the impact of having children is great in that you are living for something else, someone else. But as far as changing my lifestyle or having an impact on my lifestyle, it was a very gradual thing — that's just the way it was.

For Ellen becoming a wife and mother was inevitable, not a matter of choice. But the reality of being a mother is much harder than she envisioned. She has adjusted by pushing her husband to modify the traditional division of labor that they assumed when their marriage began. Now she works part-time and he is caretaker while she works. She perceives this to benefit each of them and the kids as well. She also has begun preparing for more involving work in the future. But her role as mother still comes first.

8

Amy

I'm the type of person who has to work.

Amy always planned to go to college and always wanted to be a teacher. She loved teaching so much that she could hardly believe she was being paid to do it. But she always planned to be a wife and mother as well. Marriage was very important to her — "marriage and not being divorced."

Her parents divorced when Amy was two. Amy had grown up in a close-knit extended family until, when she was fifteen, she moved with her mother and stepfather to Connecticut. There she was an only child in an adult-oriented household. Her mother had always worked; when Amy was younger she had spent her days with her grandmother or stepmother.

Her adolescent experiences of feeling different from her friends, who had mothers at home, and being uncomfortable in her nuclear family, make Amy want to be an at-home mother for her children. Yet, because of her commitment to and love for her career, she misses teaching very much.

Amy is a woman with commitment to a career and a strong desire to work who has chosen to follow certain "shoulds" that led her to full-time homemaking. She married and established a stereotypical division of labor with a man who prefers her to be at home with the children. She chose him over a more exciting man because she felt marriage to him would be secure and safe. As a result, Amy has been in conflict about working for the four years she has been a mother and anticipates years of conflict ahead.

Like Pam, Amy works part time, just two hours a week, but enough to feel that she is doing something career-related. Amy's conflict, however, is more acute than Pam's. While Pam feels she can change her mind if life at home gets too difficult, Amy feels too guilty about leaving the kids. Amy is in agony about an excellent full-time position she has been offered. She wants to take it but cannot envision leaving her young children.

Life with two young children is stressful for Amy. She is a devoted mother, concerned with providing enriching experiences for her daughters. Yet she needs time for herself, which is hard to get. She misses teaching, and her family misses her income.

Amy considers herself a person who has to work, not the type to stay home and clean house. Yet her commitment to being available for and involved with her kids has made her "partially sacrifice a career." This leaves her feeling constricted and conflicted, but in time she knows she will go back.

❦ ❦ ❦

I think I always just expected I would be a mother. It was just there. It was appealing. I don't think I ever questioned it. I always wanted to be a cowgirl or a waitress. I had high ambitions! There was something magical about being a waitress. Television had a big influence. Years later I got to be a waitress. My father-in-law owns a bar and restaurant. My sister-in-law was sick, and I substituted for her for the summer. After that, I never wanted to be a waitress again! It was too hard. From junior high school on, I always wanted to be a teacher, and I still do. I'm one of those few people who has found something in their life that they really want to do.

Amy, an only child, was two years old when her parents divorced. She and her mother then lived with her grandparents until her mother's remarriage three years later. Her father also remarried; he and his new wife had four children, the oldest four years younger than Amy.

Dad lived right down the street from us. I saw him often; in fact in the summers I would stay at his house during the day while my mother worked. I saw him constantly. While he was working, I would play with my brothers and sisters. I had children to play with, my friends were in the neighborhood, my stepmother took care of me if my grandmother had things to do during the day. It worked out well for her, and I was home for dinner. It was the best of a strange situation. I don't remember having any problems at all.

When she was fifteen, Amy, her mother and stepfather relocated to Connecticut. She does not remember being upset by the move.

It was so exciting; it was a whole new adventure. We used to go back and forth quite often, maybe every six or seven weeks we would go.

I have to admit my mother really handled it well. It was a very good situation. She always allowed me to see my father whenever I wanted to see him; she encouraged me to see him. She never said bad things about him. It was a very good situation; it was a healthy situation. We stayed with my grandparents and then I would go to my father's. Other members of my stepfather's family were very friendly with my father, so it was no big deal.

Her extended family, though blended, had provided a buffer between Amy and her mother, who was very strict and self-centered.

My mother was a career-minded person, very different from my grandmother. I idolized my grandmother; I never got along well with my mother. She was just a business person, and that was a very important part of her life. She liked me as a child, but she is not fond of children. She never really took an active interest in things that I did in school. My grandmother was usually the one; my mother would go if it was absolutely necessary, but my grandmother was the one. She was like a mother substitute. She was the one who usually took the interest, or made the cookies, or made the costume; whatever had to be done, she would do.

I idolized my grandmother, and I still do, but it wasn't like a conflict because we lived there for three years, and I was very small, and I idolized my grandfather also. They were a very important part of my life. But my mother and I just had a relationship where we clashed until the day I got married and left the house. We don't clash anymore, but it is still a conflict in that we are very different people, and I would like for her to take an interest in my children, which she doesn't. It's a very superficial interest. She needs me when she needs me and doesn't come to see us or bother with us unless there is something that she needs. I'm sure she feels that we have a close relationship; I don't. It's not the kind of relationship that I would like. She's not someone that I could lean on or a motherly type that I could go to. If I really needed someone to lean on with a problem, I have some very close friends, or my husband and I are very close. I would turn to them before I would go to her.

Amy's memories of her adolescence, after relocating, are very bitter.

My mother is a very domineering person, and my stepfather is exactly the opposite. My mother was the boss; he was not the father image that I hoped he would be, that my father is. It was a very difficult household. I always felt very uneasy in my own household. She made it very uncomfortable. Friends were not allowed, not that they weren't allowed, but were made to feel very uneasy in our house. We had to be quiet; we couldn't make a mess; we couldn't sit on certain chairs. If I went to someone's house, about a half-hour before she was supposed to come I was a nervous wreck, because if she ever sat out there for two minutes and I didn't see her I would hear about it when I got in the car. She was a very unbending person, and my father went along with everything that she said.

Very rarely was there anything that was geared toward me. We would go on vacations, and we would go to places that were not for me. For example, I was about thirteen or fourteen, and we went to the cape for one week, and it was a very nice place but it was more elderly, shuffleboard, no young people, very few people my age, but they just wanted to relax. There was very little consideration for me. Occasionally they would do something. I remember going to the Bronx Zoo. I think that was one of the few big deal things. I think probably once I was on my own in high school or whatever I more or less did things with friends. She was very happy to have me go to a friend's house to spend the night but never did a friend ever sleep at my house.

Things got worse for Amy when time to go to college approached.

Surprisingly enough, as everyone who knows me says, I think I was fairly well adjusted. I was a good student; I was very active in school. I think my biggest problem started when I was a junior, I can remember specifically, a junior in high school. It was about November and I can remember being very happy up until that point and then going on these crying jags. I couldn't understand why it was, I was just getting severely depressed, and this went on through high school and college because, unfortunately, I stayed home and went to college. There were a lot of things that happened to me, very strange things, and I always felt it was me. Like spending Christmas in my room. I had done something wrong — I can't even remember what it was —but I had done something that she didn't like and spent three days in my room and opened Christmas presents, I think it was January 2nd or 3rd, something like that.

Amy always knew she would go to college. Her maternal grandparents were college educated, although her parents were not. Her big disappointment was that instead of going away to college as she expected, she commuted to the local state university where she earned her bachelor's degree and, later, her master's degree.

All my life I knew I was going to go to college and just accepted the fact that I was going away to college. My mother worked at a place where two of the bosses were very close friends with my grandmother's family. They lived here and would want to finance my four years wherever I wanted to go. My mother didn't want that. The way I see it is she didn't want me to have things she didn't have. My mother always wanted to go to college, and my grandparents couldn't afford it, and she couldn't accept that. So, I said I would go to a two-year school and see if I could get a scholarship or something. She didn't want me to go away because it was an opportunity that she didn't have.

After college, Amy taught in a neighboring town.

I taught kindergarten for three years and I taught first grade for one year. I loved it. I couldn't believe that I could get paid for something that I liked so much.

Amy always expected to marry and to have a family. Her views on marriage were formed in reaction to her parents' divorce.

What was important to me was marriage and not being divorced. I have so much divorce in my family that it's pathetic, and it was very important to me that when I got married I stayed married.

She met her husband in college.

We met during the middle of my junior year in college. We married in the summer after my second year of teaching. So, we went out for four years.

I never really liked him! We met through mutual friends. He was on a date. I was dating a fellow, and we had been going out for quite a while. I just kind of became uninfatuated with him, and so I guess you could call me a little out of circulation. So a friend fixed me up with another friend, a fellow that was here from Princeton. And it happened to be a friend of Alan's, to a party, and Alan happened to be there with someone, and I was there with someone else. And that's how we got together, and everyone was friendly, and we were talking, and he asked me out. It started on Easter vacation, on spring vacation, and I had nothing else to do, so we would go to play tennis or do that type of thing. He didn't have anyone else to go out with and neither did I, so we spent a lot of time together. He liked me; I wasn't really aware of what was happening. I was just having a good time and enjoying the whole thing. This went on for quite a while.

In fact, though they had a good time together, their relationship was lacking in excitement for her — so lacking in excitement that, after dating just Alan for several years, she went out behind his back.

Many, many years before, I had a friend that I had known and was very infatuated with. And during the time that I was going out with Alan, we happened to meet on a picket line during a teacher's strike, and we struck up a friendship and a relationship again. So I was going out with him, and I was just head over heels for this other fellow, unbeknown to Alan. And very, very taken in by him, and he by me. This sounds very strange and very stupid, but I was so taken in by him, in such awe, that I figured he couldn't really (basic insecurity) really like me, and it couldn't be a lasting thing. I was always very insecure about that. And I know this sounds strange, but I just felt that Alan loved me so much that it could last. I liked him; I was comfortable with him; I loved him. There weren't bells ringing or stars shining, but I just felt that I might be a little bit more secure. I was very insecure. I just needed some stability, and I felt that Alan provided that stability. With Sam, I didn't know. I was just so taken in by everything, I wasn't sure if it would be a lasting type of thing.

Alan made her feel more secure and, having dated him for so long, she was attached to his family. Following her passion for Sam seemed too risky.

I was going out with both of them, and I was going out behind Alan's back because he would never accept the fact that I just wanted a friendly relationship. He was very domineering. Consequently, I had to sneak out behind his back. And his mother died a very untimely death — she committed suicide. She was going through the change and having a very difficult time. It was a very hard thing for me to go through, because she was more like a mother to me than my own mother. She was very accepting during the times that I was having a very hard time. She wanted me to come and live with them. She was just a very nice person, so I found her death very difficult. At that time, I felt very guilty that I was going out behind Alan's back, and his mother died and blah, blah, blah. So I stopped seeing Sam. I didn't realize how much I cared for him until after I had broken everything off. And then I decided if Alan and I were going to go on the way we were, almost like being married, very tied down, then we might as well be married.

Once they decided to marry, they bought a two-family house together.

We bought it six months before we got married. We bought it in February. It was just seven years ago yesterday. We bought this two-family house before we got married, and it was an old house, and we renovated the whole thing. We lived on one floor, and we rented the other. I moved into it in June. What happened was I had an apartment by myself, and when we finally made the decision to get married, rather than spend the money for rent I moved home again for a couple of months, and then in June, after I ended teaching, I moved into the bedroom, actually, of the apartment. It wasn't totally done over. I was getting things ready, and then in August he moved in.

It was seven years ago yesterday that his mother died, and at that point we were thinking about getting married. That kind of put a more definite note on it; we decided to get married. His father had heard about this old two-family house that was extremely cheap at the time and needed a lot of renovation, so we didn't pay an awful lot of money for it. We didn't have a lot of money to spend. So we purchased that before we got married and about the same time, this was before Alan's mother died, she wanted some place where she could vacation so his parents and Alan and I went to Rhode Island to look at some land that had been advertised in the paper. We decided to go in with them as a partnership on two lots and a cottage on one of the lots. So that actually was bought maybe eight or ten months before we got married. Like we knew we were going to get married, it was just a matter of time. One of Alan's things was to have "a certain amount of money in the bank" which he never got before we got married. So we were very involved. We had a good relationship. We have had all along a good relationship.

Amy was tied in with Alan's family economically, as well as emotionally, before they formally decided to marry.

My wedding was just what my mother wanted— what else! It was a terrible day. That's another very sad part of my life. My mother has been a thorn in my side for so long, I wonder if I will ever be able to get over it. The wedding looked good but there wasn't the warmth, or whatever, underneath. A lot of things went wrong that day, like inviting people back to the house and not having enough food. But the flowers were there and printed napkins.

Part of Amy's decision to marry Alan resulted from the way he took charge. She was insecure and needed someone who would both dominate her and love her more than she loved him. Alan's being that way made her feel safe.

In the beginning we worked together, and we worked for things. We always got along well. We rarely fought. It was over money probably or some silly thing, but we never really argued. He is like a stabilizing factor. He's fairly easygoing, yet he's more in the dominating father image or something. And we got along well. But now, especially in the past couple of years, we've grown really closer. We know what each other is thinking, and we know how we're feeling, and we do things. I was in a way very selfish. He was always doing things for me, was always very thoughtful. He really loved me much more than I loved him.

Her description of Alan contrasts sharply with her description of her stepfather.

I couldn't stand my stepfather. He was a nice person but he just turned my stomach; he just absolutely turned my stomach. I can remember thinking of him as a little mouse and her as a tyrant. He was the type of person that if I did something wrong, it was not where the mother is at home and said, "Wait till your father gets home," it was, "Wait until your mother gets home." If he had once stood up to me and said, "That really

wasn't a good thing to do, we're disappointed" and so on....
He had no backbone as far as that was concerned, and I just
couldn't respect him for that. She's very domineering and he's
just, "yes dear, yes dear," that type of thing. That just gnawed
on me even more and made my life even more miserable. He
was kind to me but I just objected to his character.

Although Amy was not madly in love with Alan, she obviously liked his domineering character.

As newlyweds, Amy and Alan were very busy, each working full time, she taking graduate school classes, and together
renovating their house. Finances were tight, but they had a good
time.

> Alan wasn't making that much. Like I said, we bought this
> old home and the whole thing had to be done over — two new
> kitchens, two new bathrooms. He wasn't making that much,
> and for a period of time he was unemployed. We had bills. The
> first couple of years that we were married — when I think
> about it now we must have been screwballs — we went out a
> lot, we did a lot of things, we took a lot of trips, short trips,
> nothing big deal, but we just enjoyed ourselves. We never
> saved a lot of money ever and to this day we don't, but we
> managed to get by.

Amy really liked being married; it made her feel that she
finally had a family.

> It wasn't until I got married that I really understood what
> my problem was, why I was so envious of people. It was their
> family. I never had a family. That's what my whole problem
> was, and it wasn't until then that I could see it. I think once I
> realized that that's what my problem was, I realized that many
> times families aren't all they're cracked up to be. Like he has
> a brother, and he has a sister, and they get together for holi-
> days, but they're not close. I started to really think things out
> more logically to myself, and I don't get those fits of depression
> any more. And Alan has really realized that my mother is a
> problem. She really is a very strange person, and he resents
> her very much for not liking the kids and being a grandparent
> to the kids and so forth. I think knowing that it's not me that's

really having all the problems, we've become emotionally much closer, and I realize that I really do love him. I've grown to love him, to depend on him. We have a good marriage. I still don't see stars, but I'm happy.

At the time of the interviews, Amy was thirty-one, Alan was thirty-two, Patty was four and Rachel was two. Amy was a homemaker and taught reading improvement two hours a week at a local university, and Alan was an appraiser for the state.

A little over a year after they married, during Amy's fourth year of teaching, they decided to have a baby.

We always wanted children; we just always knew we would have children. I had been teaching for four years at the time, and I really loved it. But it was a very difficult time —in three years we'd been through two strikes, and I worked in a school that was very rough and had a lot of very bad incidents down there, guns and knives. At the end of the fourth year there were a lot of problems, and I just felt that I needed a break from it, and I wanted to have children, and I felt this was the time to take a break and have them. He was as excited about it as I was. We both wanted children very much, and the timing was right.

The pregnancy positively affected their marriage.

I was very happy, excited. I was a princess. It was again one of those things that brought us closer together. Neither one of my pregnancies were actually beauties. With Rachel[her second child] I had a very difficult time. In the first three months of my pregnancy with Patty[her first] I was very sick. I had just morning sickness, and I was extremely sick, and I was working at the time. It was difficult. I managed through the custodian's help at school — getting there early to open the door — having bathroom doors open to run in and be sick and run back. It was tough. It lasted for about three and a half months, and my principal was very patient. At the time I was teaching first grade, so they were very excited and very patient. The class was an experiment; this was our second year together. I had had them in kindergarten and then we all moved to first grade, so it was a very special year for all of us, and I had had many of their brothers and sisters, and we were all, like a family, excited about it.

Once the school year was over, Amy relaxed and enjoyed her pregnancy, although she had typical complaints, especially at the end.

I don't know how to pinpoint it, but it was a nice feeling, maybe feeling feminine. It was a very feminine womanly feeling, and I enjoyed that. But at the end, I hardly felt feminine with Patty — I was a little elephant. I had a good time with Patty. I got to do things, and I had some time. I took courses that I never had the opportunity to take before. I had always been taking school courses, required courses, and I took a lot of sewing courses and pottery courses and things I just enjoyed doing. Alan and I did a lot of things — this was when I was pregnant with Patty — we did a lot of things together, to sort of make the time go by. I enjoyed that.

I disliked the normal uncomfortable feelings and was fat, very fat. I wouldn't have another child. One of the reasons is that I would not want to be pregnant. The thing is what it does to my poor body. At this point, I don't think my body could stand it. I don't want to be fat and chubby any more.

With Amy not working and the added expenses of a new baby, finances, never easy, became more strained.

I think finances have always been a concern. We've never had it easy. We still don't have it easy. At the time, I was making more than Alan, as a matter of fact. It was a big deal. He worries about finances all the time. At the time, I was making more than he was, but again we were living in a house that we owned, and we worked on getting rent from downstairs. So it was tough. After we had Patty, now that I remember, there was a time when we were really hurting for money. It was difficult. It was a financial strain for us. We went for almost a year without going out to dinner. We had to sacrifice a lot.

Once the baby was born, Amy missed working more than she had expected.

During the time I was pregnant, because that was my summer vacation from teaching, I really hadn't gotten the feeling of not working. It was a very traumatic experience for me, in fact it still is. I just adored teaching, and it's just something that I had always wanted to do. I loved it; it was just a very positive experience, and it was very difficult for me, especially at the beginning when Patty was a tiny baby and didn't require a lot of care and time. She was sleeping so much that I would just run around the house — what do I do with myself? I could be doing this, I could be helping this one, I could be doing that, and it has always been difficult for me to give up that kind of career. That's why I have always pursued something part time.

Leaving her career was harder than Amy anticipated.

I don't think I really thought it out. I always thought it was something to hold on to, that once they got to be five years old I would go back to teaching. Now I see that that's a lot different, and I don't think I feel quite that same way. But I knew in my mind that I would be coming back — don't worry, I'll be back.

Amy actually returned to work long before Patty was five years old.

Number one, we needed some extra money. Number two, I missed it so much. When Patty was eleven months old, I had been tutoring. This was not really working: I helped out a friend tutoring a child in reading. I hadn't completed my masters at the time, I almost had, and the child made a great deal of progress and to that point had had a lot of problems in reading for seven or eight years, up until seventh or eight grade. So the head of the reading department of that system called me and wanted to know what the magic formula was. So I went in to talk to him, and they offered me a job. I was very flattered because jobs were very scarce, and I was getting two or three job offers a week from systems all over. I had just enough experience. I was a reading consultant or a reading teacher. I had four years of experience, and they didn't want any more because they didn't want to pay for it, so I was getting loads of job offers. I was very flattered by the whole thing. That kind of appeased me for a while, but then when this actual confrontation came and it was right around the corner from my house, I thought well the money was very good, and I thought, "I'll try it." Also, I think what made me decide to try it was Alan's cousin who lived a block away from me had a young child and needed some extra money. She was a very loving person, and she was more than willing to take care of Patty, who was eleven months old at the time. I would be out of school by two-thirty, so it didn't seem too bad.

She relied on Alan's cousin to provide care for Patty, but felt very guilty. So when the job fell through, she was relieved but still in conflict.

I would leave the house at eight, and I could pick her up at two-thirty. She slept a lot of the time, and she'd be with another young child, and our cousin was very kind, so I thought this might ease our financial burden for a while. So I told them I would do it on a temporary basis to see how it worked out. If it worked out, then I would finalize the contract. Well, what they were actually doing was waiting for a niece of the super-intendent to graduate from college; it was a political job. I did it for about three months, but I felt very guilty about leaving Patty with someone else. I was still taking courses so that on Thursdays I would pick her up at two-thirty, I would bring her home and play with her for half an hour, although I was totally exhausted, and then another sitter would come in and watch her while I ran off, zipped something in the oven, and zipped off to class. I wouldn't be home until ten at night. It was tough. I enjoyed the teaching, so it wasn't that tough on me at the time, but I felt guilty about Patty. My mother had always worked when I was little, and I felt that I missed out on a lot of things, and I didn't want that to happen to mine. So I quit. We reversed our situation. I took care of my cousin's child, and she went off to work. That went on for a while, and then she was laid off. Then I guess a year or so after that I didn't really work. I didn't do anything. But it has always been a conflict. I love teaching. I've done other teaching, but teaching little children is what I like to do. So it's still a hassle, and here it is four or five years later, and I think it will always be a hassle.

Alan was not in favor of Amy working.

Although we needed the money and although he wanted to have the money to help out, he also had mixed feelings because he felt that I should be home with the children. We think the same way in our philosophy of child-raising. He had mixed emotions also. We needed the money, I was happy, I liked what I was doing, but I should be home with them.

In order to minimize her time away from teaching, Amy had her second child two years after Patty was born.

We planned this one also in terms of I would like to go back to work someday, so I didn't want a great span between children. So it was very important to me to have this child at this time.

Amy's second pregnancy was fraught with problems.

With Patty it was trying to keep the weight down. With Rachel, from a week after I learned that I was pregnant until the moment I had her, it was one constant problem after another. They still say that Rachel was the baby that never should have been.

A week after I found out I was pregnant I started showing, and I went to the doctor. They said that I would lose the baby, and they gave me the instructions of what I was supposed to do when it happened. So we waited for I don't know how many weeks — it seemed like months and months and months. It was a couple of months, and this kept going on. Nothing happened. I didn't have all the nausea I had with Patty, but I just wasn't feeling well and was very concerned. I did resign myself to the fact that if this baby was not meant to be, it wasn't meant to be. I wanted to lose it in the beginning rather than waiting all this long time.

After about three months, they decided that things looked a little bit better, and I had stopped showing, so they decided to give me the regular blood tests that they give you when you're pregnant. When they did, they found that I had taxoplasmosis. It's a blood condition that causes deformed and retarded babies. It does not affect the pregnant woman but if you contracted it within the first three months of your pregnancy, when your baby's brain or bones or whatever were forming, then it's very serious. If you contracted it in the seventh, eight, or ninth, or anytime after that month of pregnancy, then it may not be a problem at all. Well, I had a slight case when I had Patty, and the doctor hadn't even mentioned it to me because it wasn't important. I had gotten it somewhere along the line. You get it from raw or very rare meat or cat feces.

So I had this, so I had to have test after test done. I had to keep going back. I went to the doctor once a week for most of the pregnancy and had to keep having loads of blood tests. They had to send them to Hartford and cultures had to grow. You waited from one week to the next for them to tell you something. And I had it in a very high degree. So we had to sit down with the doctor, and we had to consider what we were going to do. She was very practical, and she wanted to know what my feelings would be if the baby was deformed or retarded. She would like me to make a decision ahead of time, rather than an emotional decision if the baby was born alive. That was a very traumatic experience, and I had to live with it for the total time of my pregnancy. I had one glorious week of being pregnant and from then on it was downhill. And it was very important to me because I wanted my children fairly close.

About the seventh or eight month, very early, I started having contractions and going into labor and, in the meantime, I was putting on no weight. I had put on a couple of pounds. The baby was very tiny and wasn't developing, and they were very concerned at this point. They said the baby would be premature, and it would be so tiny that they doubted that it would be alive or would survive. So I lived for a couple more months knowing that any day it would be time this baby could come.

Rachel ended up being two weeks late and completely normal. I had to be induced, and she was perfectly healthy. They gave her test after test — she was like a pin cushion. They gave her so many tests, and she was a perfectly normal baby, and they couldn't believe it.

Amy took a baby-care course before Patty was born, but not childbirth preparation classes with Alan. She was interested in learning to care for her infant but, like many local women, did not want to think about the delivery.

> I took a lot of the baby courses offered at the hospital, and I was just very excited about having a baby. It was a very big deal; Alan and I were both ecstatic. I would block out of my mind the actual process of birth, because I didn't want to think that it might be a little scary. I was perhaps a little bit anxious, but it wasn't of major concern to me. I had a lot of faith in my doctor, and that's what kept me going.
>
> Alan went on the tour; he didn't actually take the classes with me, but there is one evening session where the husband goes in with you, and he did. It was very funny because that was at the time when the husband going in to watch the birth was getting to be a very big deal. He went on this tour, and it was a hot summer night and five or six couples were with us, and they're showing us around. They walked into the delivery room, and there's no one there, just a very sterile delivery room, and he had to sit down. He turned whiter than a sheet. They're showing all the things and what happens, and he got very woozy about the whole thing.
>
> He was with me during labor, but he did not go in with me. My doctor wasn't there — she doesn't work on weekends — so another doctor delivered, and she felt a little funny about having him there, so he didn't go in.

Amy's doctor was not available for her first delivery, and things did not go smoothly. During the second delivery her doctor took charge.

> When I had Patty, I had a peridural. My doctor was away, and I was in total shock that she was not going to be there. I was in a lot of pain, and so she wanted to relieve me. She didn't know me, and I didn't know her, so she gave me this very early, and she did an awful lot of cutting. And evidently, from my doctor's standpoint, did not do a very good job. I had hemorrhoids and had to sit on pillows. It was very painful for about two and a half weeks after that. So with Rachel, my doctor wanted to avoid this whole thing. So she has this midwife

giving me these breathing instructions each time I go for a visit. She says you do these and practice these, and I say oh sure, sure, sure, and I never really practice them because with Patty I didn't have to do anything. I was totally conscious and there was no problem. They did all the pushing, and I had a very easy time, so I figure well, she's going to do this again. So I didn't really pay any attention to all the breathing exercises. However, I thought that I was going to have the peridural and probably would have gone out of my mind if I ever knew at the time that I wasn't going to have it. Right up until the last minute I thought she was going to give it to me, and I kept waiting and waiting. I'm very glad that she didn't tell me, because I would have been fearful. The midwife kept saying now breathe — I hadn't practiced any of this — so I'm doing them and that was it.

In contrast to most mothers, especially to most local mothers, Amy's mother helped only on the day that Amy came home from the hospital with Patty. This was in keeping with Amy's complaint that her mother and stepfather do not relate to the children like interested grandparents. Amy's friends and husband helped more.

She took the day off from work, and she wanted to do some clothes shopping for fall. So she stayed the day. I had girlfriends that came over, and they really helped.

This was again the case when Amy came home from the hospital with Rachel.

My mother was there when I got home. She was probably there for the day but that was about it. I think Alan probably took a couple of days off from work. We tried to make it as natural as possible for Patty. She was two years and two months old at the time and had never been separated from me, and we knew that the fact that I was away was tough on her.

Amy chose not to breastfeed her babies.

It just wasn't something for me, and I felt that I should feel comfortable with it. I didn't eat properly, and I don't know — I'm too modest a person, I think that might be it. I was pressured in a sense, very pressured, by a lot of friends and a cousin of Alan's who's a very active person in LaLeche, and it was just the thing to do. Alan wanted me to try, but I just didn't feel comfortable.

She felt more prepared for motherhood than she might have been, but certainly not fully prepared.

When I was working I was teaching little children, and I think that gave me a lot of experience dealing with children. It didn't come as a shock to me or as a totally new thing as it might to someone who was a secretary or in another profession. But I was never around little babies. The only contact that I had was my teaching years; I can't remember any experiences before I actually started teaching. I had very little contact with small babies. And they never tell you about all the unpleasant things, that you'll be up all night, and the problems.

Though Amy likes infants, she was not that fond of routine infant care.

I like little babies; they're so cuddly and cute. I really enjoyed it. What I liked the least were the routine things like changing diapers and perhaps feeding, although that wasn't really awful. I had two little girls that ate anything, so it wasn't unpleasant as with some children. I liked to play with them and enjoy them. I was very impatient. I just couldn't wait until they got to their next stage so that I could try this out or see if they could do this or that.

After the babies were born Amy was home and Alan was working. She was the primary caretaker, although Alan would pitch in when needed.

I did everything when I was home during the day. When he came home, he would often change them. He would take over if I had to go to the store, go grocery shopping, or if I wanted to go out. He would feed them; he really likes that. He would take over right where I left off. He'd give them a bottle. When I had Patty, I was really very sore, and it was difficult for me, so he would really help out, but as soon as I got on my feet and felt much better, after a couple of weeks, then I would try to feed her at night because he had to get up and go to work, and I would nap when Patty napped. We're a very fifty-fifty type of family —one helped the other when the other was in need.

This was consistent with their general approach to dividing responsibilities. From the beginning of their marriage, even though they both worked full time, cooking, cleaning, and laundry were Amy's responsibilities, but Alan was willing to help.

In the very beginning he helped me out because I wasn't a very good cook, and then I kind of took over. I needed help in the kitchen because I hadn't practically ever cooked before. He was tolerant. We joke about it. I would put on a meal, and I would have meat, then we'd have potatoes for dessert. Then we'd have Rolaids. I could never coordinate; each thing always came out one after the other. But then I would get home earlier, so I would try things out.

Alan still helps, especially with the laundry. Amy both appreciates his assistance and worries that it reflects her own shortcomings.

I'm so ashamed. If I'm behind, or there is something that he would really like and hasn't had for a week or so, like a flannel shirt, and hasn't seen it around, then he'll probably put a load of laundry in so he can get it. I'm pretty good — sometimes I just get bogged down, and he'll help out. He helps fold the clothes. I purposely leave laundry baskets around the house. He does it quite often. It's not a routine but sometimes I'll put a wash in late in the day, and if that happens to be around when he gets home he'll fold it. I usually try to get things done early in the morning. He's been doing it an awful lot lately, but he doesn't mind. If he minded, he wouldn't do it.

Laundry is the chore Alan most often helps with, but he also sometimes makes sandwiches or Sunday breakfast, rinses the dishes for the dishwasher, or reads the bedtime story. In her absence, he would do anything. Amy considers him a very helpful husband. He works long hours, however, and that is stressful for her.

His regular work hours are nine to five, but he also tends bar at his father's restaurant Friday evenings and Saturday afternoons. Friday night is different because he works on Friday nights. He's home for about half an hour, and I give him a quick dinner, and then we have a neighborhood thing with three families where all the other husbands work late and so we all get together, and we all have two children. We take turns at different houses. Now, unfortunately, Alan's the one that doesn't come because he doesn't get home until like one-thirty. Six-thirty, seven, seven-thirty, the other two husbands will pop in, and we feed them. But it's nice, because it's otherwise a kind of lonely, trying day, especially on Friday. Friday is the end of the week. In the beginning, when we were first married, I found it very lonely because when we were dating we always went out on Friday nights. Then when we got married, it was such a disappointment on Friday to come home from school.

On Saturday he leaves about eleven-thirty, and he gets home around five-thirty on Saturday night. So, Saturday is like another day for me with the children. We've been discussing now perhaps every other Saturday would work out a little better. His father really depends on him, but it's a cramp. I find it very irritating, him working six days a week.

Alan is the breadwinner. They also have some income from their property and her part-time job. Alan pays the bills, but Amy has free access to their money.

Our income is about thirty-one thousand a year. If I want money, or I need money, I just take it. I'm usually pretty good about money. Occasionally I'll just go on a spree, and if I go shopping for myself, I may go a little over and buy two pairs of slacks instead of one pair of slacks.

Alan's father also provides a substantial amount of food for their table.

> We get a lot of our meat given to us, which is really nice. Alan's father comes over every Tuesday, and he will give us perhaps an eye of the round, a couple pounds of hamburg, a pound of bacon, a pound of butter. I try to allot it so that I can stretch as much of the week's meat around that, so I really have to buy very little meat.

Although their family income is not high, things seem comfortable in comparison with earlier times.

> Right now we're in fairly good shape, so we don't have a lot of really heavy worries about money. We have a savings account, so that we can't get really caught short if we needed it. We're not living high on the hog, but it's not quite so bad now. We used to have discussions about money all the time — it's the only friction we ever had, over money. Especially the point where I was home with Patty, and we weren't able to go out that much because we didn't have that much money. I think it was harder for me because at least he got out during the day. I couldn't get out because we didn't have that much money to do anything.

Amy feels very strongly that good parents need to have interests independent from their children. She works part time and is once again considering full-time work.

> I can remember my pediatrician saying to me that parents, in order to be good parents, have to have some time and some interests for themselves, to be a person in and of themselves, along with being a parent. You can live for your children and that doesn't necessarily make you a person because you are so involved with them you don't have other interests. I see many mothers who are so totally involved with their children, and they get really crabby and yell at them. That's not necessarily a good household because they're with them all the time. Many mothers will condemn the working mother, but there are those people who need to be away from their children some time during the day. I think, as someone once said, it's

not the quantity of time but it's the quality of the time that you put in it. So I think parents have to have their own life also.

Right now I'm going through a very big conflict. I was offered an exceptional job, and it would double our income. It's a full-time job, nine to five. It's a very difficult choice for me to make because it's a once-in-a-lifetime opportunity, possibly. It's a very attractive job, but the fact that I would be gone for so much of the time is disturbing to me, especially when they are so young. So I guess I am more, at this point, leaning towards the children. I would like very much at least to work more of a part-time job. I don't know if I'm being too over-protective. I would like very much to take the job. It's doubling our salary; I would be making more than he would. I'd like very much to do it; it's a tremendous opportunity. I don't have to do it for the rest of my life. I could do it for two years, and we could get on our feet, and then I could leave if I want, or if it works out really well and I have the children in school— but I don't know if I'm being too over-protective or what type of situation it will be for them. I'm the type of person that I do have to work, not because I have to but because I want to.

As much as Amy wants the job, she does not want to be away from her children. Alan has negative feelings about her taking the job. Rather than offering to share household responsibilities to enable her to work, he expresses concern that she will be overworked. His father is against her working, though she is encouraged by her mother and friends. Unfortunately, her mother has not served as a positive model of a working mother for Amy.

Alan feels strongly that it's my decision, but he doesn't want me to get over my head with something, to be burdened with the responsibility of the house, to be worrying about the kids. He would like me to take the job very much, but on the other hand, I think he's swaying a little more against it for the simple reason that it might be too much for me to handle, not so far as the job but as far as the total. It also puts an added burden on him. He would not work on weekends any more; we would just have weekends to each other.

As far as family is concerned, Alan's father is definitely against it: I should be home with the kids from now until doomsday. He's expressed his opinion to us many times when I've done different things. My mother is entirely opposite, of course. She's bugging me about this job, more for the material things we could get from this. As far as friends, a good many of my friends work part time. They are either a nurse or a teacher. Or, if they're not doing anything, I find that they want to, and they're envious of me because I am doing something. I heard so many people that I was very surprised at, whose children are getting to be school age, who want to go out and work. So I don't feel any negative pressure from friends.

YetAmy prides herself on how she and Alan are raising their children differently from how she was raised, and that is connected to her being home with their kids.

I am here; I am home with them; I'm interested in them. Not that my mother didn't or doesn't love me, but I think that they have a better sense of well-being, of a family situation, of being loved, of being secure, of knowing that we're here and want to do things for them. I think that's different than what I had.

Very rarely did my parents do anything that was geared towards me. I don't know if we're going off on the other extreme; my husband and I spend a lot of time with the children. In fact, we are having a discussion about whether we should start doing some things for ourselves and more towards ourselves. Whereas, my mother was just the opposite.

Within the context of her devotion to being home with the children, Amy consciously strives for some time for herself.

I like to take an hour for myself, but it never seems to work out that way. I get cranky if I don't get my time. I have a soap opera that I like to watch occasionally, or read a book, or maybe just lay down.

We try to put Rachel in for a nap and, if not, try at least to have her go into her room for an hour and play in there. Patty, I occupy her with her puzzles or Play-Doh or something. I've tried to tell her that I would like a time all to myself, that I need a rest. We haven't quite got this one hour period or half-hour period down-pat yet. Nobody quite understands that Mommy needs a little bit of time.

Not surprisingly, with two preschoolers she rarely manages to get any time for herself, which causes her stress.

I get along well with them. There are times when I get discouraged — when I get tired or when I don't have any time to myself. You can't go to the bathroom in privacy. You can't do anything in privacy. I think that's what gets me irritated, makes me fly off the handle at them. It's usually when I really feel pressured — if they'd just leave me alone for a few minutes — but generally we get along. What irritates me is that I want to be alone for a few minutes, and they can't respect that, they are just not old enough. They just don't respect my wish and that's usually what's a conflict, whether it's over something else or not, it's usually that was the initial problem to begin with. I do try to entertain them. By five o'clock Alan comes home, and I just die.

Like most of the women I spoke with, Amy finds motherhood more demanding than she expected, but extremely rewarding as well.

It's not easy being a parent. It brings a lot of joy, and I think more often, if you have a healthy child, the good outweighs the bad. I'm thinking particularly of a girl I know. It's a conflict in their marriage because he wants children and she does not. It's a very difficult thing because she is a teacher, she gets enough of kids every day and she would be very miserable, and I respect her for that. I think I would miss something; I would really miss a part of my life if I couldn't have children. I really want them. But she doesn't feel that way, and that's fine. I respect her for that.

Amy feels that having a family has enhanced her marriage and given her what she had always missed.

It's brought Alan and I closer together. We have a lot of things in common now. We've really enjoyed them. It's something that we've always wanted. We just took it for granted because we've always wanted to have children. It's given new meaning to our lives since our marriage. For me, it's kind of finalized the family that I didn't have.

There are the professional costs and personal conflicts about working, but they have not made her regret having children.

There are times when I really would like to teach, but I wouldn't think of doing it for a minute really—some days, maybe— but I wouldn't. Parenting is something that I wanted and I am very happy. I think being a parent you have to sacrifice a lot of things. I had to partially sacrifice a career, but in time I'll go back.

In fifteen years Amy expects to be working. In fact, she expects to be working much sooner than that, but she still feels conflicted about it.

I would be working. Again, I want to be here. They probably need you as much at seventeen as they do at five. But I think I would be the type of person where, even if I had a full-time job, I'd be involved with them so it wouldn't be too bad if I were out working or doing something. I'm not the type to stay home and clean house and I do have a skill and I enjoy it.

Amy is in acute conflict. She knows that she is not at her best at home with the kids all day; she knows that with cooperation from her husband she could handle both employment and motherhood. She would enjoy both the work and the money. She has a good education, career experience, and commitment to her career, but her choice of a traditional marriage limits her options. Alan does not support her working, and she feels guilty about leaving her children. She has been pushed by traditional expectations to give up teaching, which she enjoys so much and which pays more than her husband earns, for full-time motherhood. Amy chose to marry Alan in part because of his traditionally masculine, domineering qualities and so accepts his control. Her life is full of contradictions as a result of her commitment to both career and motherhood.

9

Janet

I like knowing that I've overcome the big change.

Janet was second born in a working-class family with nine children. While Janet lived at home, her father worked as a salesman and drank a lot. Her mother cared for the large brood and "took care of everything." Her father's drinking and the constant stream of babies made family life difficult for Janet.

Like Ellen and most working-class girls, Janet dreamed her life would be transformed by a marriage unlike that of her parents. She and her husband would always be madly in love, each would have a career, and they would have wonderful children, a house, a car, vacations, etc. Marriage was important; motherhood was secondary, since she knew what a burden it had been for her mother.

She was set to attend state college in the fall after her high school graduation when an accidental pregnancy changed her plans. Janet was one of two women I interviewed who became pregnant at their high school proms. Janet had an abortion; the other woman had the baby. But both gave up their plans for higher education as a result. Janet's family opposed abortion and provided no assistance. She went to work to earn money to pay for the procedure and was left on her own at the age of eighteen.

At her job Janet met and fell in love with a man twelve years older than herself who already had two children. In spite of her parents' objections, she lived with, became pregnant by, and married him. But the reality of her young marriage and infant did not match her dream; the marriage lasted less than two years. During that time finances necessitated that she work full time while she struggled to adjust to new motherhood. Her mother-in-law cared for the baby while Janet worked.

Janet is divorced, working full time, and living with a man about her age. Away from the tensions of the difficult marriage, she has finally adjusted to motherhood. Janet feels that being a mother has forced her to be more responsible, which makes her proud. In her new relationship she has attained some financial and emotional comfort and a shared division of labor. She plans never to have another child unless she can take at least a year off from work after it is born.

I was going to marry somebody who was very handsome and very rich. It was one of those happy-ever-after things, but I never really thought that there was going to be anything else. I'd get married and live happily ever after. Always be in love, madly in love with my husband and he'd be madly in love with me and we'd have wonderful little children and a wonderful new life, and eventually we'd have a house and a car and take vacations and do this and that. And I'd have my career and he'd have his career. I was wishing that. You learn as you grow up that things don't go as you plan.

Being a mother was secondary to being happy. It was because I had been part mother growing up. We had to take care of kids; we knew what a drag it was for my mother.

Second born of nine children, Janet had a lot of childcare responsibilities while growing up, as well as a lot of concern for her mother because of her father's heavy drinking. Her father had finally given up drinking three years before we spoke.

He drank, which was horrible because he was one of those mean drunks. You were scared all the time he was drunk, which was most of the time from noon till we went to bed. There was a lot of tension there because we were afraid of saying or doing the wrong thing. He is much better, from what I understand, now that he isn't drinking.

My father always seemed too concerned with himself. He never helped out with the kids except in disciplinary things. He was always drinking. I do admire the fact that he finally, after twenty-some years, gave it up. That's the only thing I can say I admire about him. My mother had tremendous problems in her marriage with my father, but rather than talk about them, face them, when her kids are running away from home and all upset about it, she would just appeal to their feelings towards her to make things go smoothly. She wouldn't ever admit that, "Yes, your father is a drunk. Yes, we're having difficulties, he hit me. Yes, this is a bad situation but it's a situation that has to happen because that's how it's supposed to be — married forever." She never came out and said, "I love this man regardless of what you may think or what he does." She had all the responsibility, all the hassles, all the heartache, but she never drank, and she took care of everything, made everything go smoothly for him. If there was a problem she'd hear about it, but she wouldn't want him to find out. She kept everything from him, so that he wouldn't explode, or so there was no tension. She took all this pressure on herself, and they never shared anything.

He'd be drunk and just want to beat somebody. My mother, of course, would end up getting smacked because she got in the way. They disagreed, I think, on financial things, because my father would want to go out and buy something that was totally unnecessary, just to make himself happy — some new gadget, camera, TV or radio or something. My mother would say, "Listen, we need food. We got to pay the utilities." He was just sort of selfish.

The large family struggled to make ends meet on her father's salesman salary. He had attended college but never earned a degree. Her mother had a nursing degree but, with so many children to care for, worked only occasionally as a waitress or factory worker.

I always had a part-time job. I started working when I was sixteen. It all went to my family until I moved out of the house. Mostly waitressing — it was all you could get — evenings and after school. I resented a lot of it. There was one point in my junior year that I was working three part-time jobs plus going to high school. I saved enough for school, but it seemed like every time something came up it was gone. It was borrowed or you know.

My parents inherited some money when I turned eighteen, which was a weird thing. My grandfather died then, and his brother had money and had died like three months before, so all his money had already gone through probate and was given to my grandfather who gave it to my father within a real short amount of time. Close to a million. It made a big change. I can see the difference in the younger kids. They went and bought a house, paid cash for it, bought a cottage, bought a boat, went on trips. And my father drank and drank and drank and drank. He made all sorts of bad investments. By that time I was out.

Although growing up was hard in her large, working-class family, Janet's relationships with her sisters helped her to cope. The four oldest siblings were girls, all born within three and a half years of each other.

I had the four of us. We fought a lot, like sisters do, but we were open with each other enough where we would discuss what was happening and we'd voice our opinions, our worries, what we hated, and what we liked, and we talked enough about it that it wasn't like one of us worrying about something. If we were worried, we would talk about it amongst ourselves, and then find out that everybody was worried about something.

What I remember with the most pleasure is just the sisters. I mean I can also remember them with the most pain, too. But it was fun; we lived in a nice little house and in a nice little area and we got along well together. We were friends. We've sort of separated but we're still friends; we still would talk about anything.

Janet left home when she was only seventeen.

My parents moved when I was in my senior year, and I stayed with an aunt because it was just ridiculous — it was in February after midyears, and I had been in the Wallingford school system since kindergarten and felt I might as well finish here. My mother's sister moved down the side of town that the high school was at so I could walk from there.

I was going to go to college. I'd been accepted at Central, but I had an abortion, and I had to pay for it, and I couldn't go to school. I was pregnant. I got pregnant at my senior prom. You really realize when it's only once that it happens.

My family knew about the abortion. I had it on a Sunday. The Thursday before that I had to tell my mother, which was a weird situation. A woman who was a very close friend worked at the laboratory where my urine test came in and threatened to tell her. She called me in. It was like, you should tell your mother — she's going to find out. It was like saying, if you don't tell her, I will. So here I am real shook up about this whole thing, and the thought of telling my mother is like... but I did and she was great about it.

You can see from her history she's anti-abortion. She did say that she would do anything to help me if I decided not to have an abortion. I couldn't see saddling her with a tenth kid, which would be what it would boil down to. I couldn't. We both knew that I was making the right decision; at the time it seemed like the only decision.

I have had two abortions. This first one, my dreadful experience, was right after the abortion laws were changed and we had to go to New York. I was seventeen. I had to wait till I was eighteen in my home state, that was the big thing, so I could do it without parental consent. I'll never forget what an experience that was. It was a clinic set up just for that, and there were women and girls from all over the country. It was like musical chairs.

The second one I had right after my husband left, which was totally different. I think they're much more concerned with your feelings now, whether or not you can actually deal with it. You go into counseling now, and they tell you exactly what's happening. It's just entirely different. It was a different experience.

Although Janet's mother was "great" about the news that Janet needed an abortion, she was very concerned with protecting the family from embarrassment.

She didn't want anybody to know about my pregnancy, so she covered it up and never talked about it. She wanted things to go smoothly and if there was any embarrassment that was always going to be hushed up. She didn't want anybody talking about her family or her life. When things got really bad, and people did start talking about it, she would just like close up. She still does that.

As a result, it was years before Janet really understood her mother's feelings about her abortion.

We were talking about my abortion, and this was like the first time we had talked about it in three, four years. She said that when she was pregnant with Lisa — she'd already had five kids, they didn't have enough money for another kid, enough room in the house for another kid, and she's pregnant again — she tried to give herself an abortion. She said, you'll never understand what fears a person goes through after they've done something to themselves and done something horrible. She was so worried through the rest of her pregnancy that she had done something to damage the kid. After she had the kid she kept waiting for something to happen that would be a direct result of what she had tried to do. She went through years of agony over that, which I didn't even know about. She said, "Of course, when you said you were going to do it I was like, 'Oh, my God, she has to go through the agony I went through.'" But she could understand that I had to do it.

In spite of the fact that she had an abortion and not a baby, Janet's high school pregnancy changed the course of her life. Instead of attending college as she had planned, she got a job to pay for the abortion and moved into an apartment of her own.

I met Ken while I was working. My parents had just moved to Madison. I fell in love, the whole bit. He was separated, getting a divorce. He was a chef at the restaurant I was working at at the time. This took a couple of years, but he moved in with me, and then my parents just flipped. They didn't want me to have anything to do with him. He had been married, and he was too old for me. I get pregnant, and I intended to marry this man, but I don't have enough money to pay for the hospital or the baby because he's doling out so much money in support of his other family. I asked my parents if they could help, and my father refused even though they had gotten this big bundle. I couldn't get welfare. I couldn't get any help from anybody. I didn't even have a bed for this baby to sleep in.

What happened was I finally said to Ken he's going to tell her [his ex-wife] we can't give her all this money a week, not until I get back to work full time. What happened was I had a full-time and a part-time job, and the part-time one was where I'm working now full time. I was working at a restaurant waitressing up until July twenty-fifth, and I had him on the thirty-first. I still had the part-time job, and I just called in sick when I went to the hospital. I went back to the part-time one that Wednesday when he and I came home on Sunday. It was right down the stairs from where I lived, so I just brought him down with me. When he was nine weeks old, I got another full-time job where I didn't want to be. I was working seven days a week, laundering at a convalescent hospital.

At the time of the interviews, Janet was twenty-five years old and her son, Johnny, was three. She was divorced from Ken, who was thirty-seven and working as a chef. She lived with Steve, who was twenty-seven and worked at a print shop. He was divorced and had no children. They had recently moved into a very nice two-bedroom apartment in a lovely neighborhood.

Janet and Ken had lived together for a year before she got pregnant.

Johnny was no mistake. We decided. Actually he decided, and I was so in love I decided too. God knows why he decided, because as soon as I got pregnant it was like he didn't really care. But I can't say that he convinced me and I didn't really want to. I figured it was time, we were in love, things were going to be okay. Plus, I felt that old thing where his other wife had kids, why I'm going to be just as important — the mother of his child — which is a very bad reason to have a kid.

Ken was separated but married still. It was difficult because his wife wasn't really too happy with the idea of the separation, much less me when I came into the picture. He got divorced in April before Johnny was born, and we were married in June. Johnny was born in July.

Our relationship got very strained after I had the baby. It was not very good before that either because he was very jealous. He's an awful person. We lost all communication somewhere along the line. I'm not sure exactly where. I haven't ever been able to pinpoint it, but it was during the time we were trying to get pregnant. It's like we were putting pressure on each other, plus my family pressure, and his wife, and, oh God, his kids. Everything was just a little too much. There were things about each other that we hassled over until it got to the point where we'd keep things from each other, and we weren't open any more. I hassled over his ex-wife things. He wanted complete control over me. Which was another reason why I wanted to get pregnant.

I think I had a child to fill some kind of empty gap. I had him because I was in love, and I figured this is what you should do. But I also had him to fill a loneliness that I was experiencing because he was always going to visit his children, and I didn't have my own child. I couldn't understand how he felt about his without having one of my own. I had it because there was that loneliness there. I also had it to prove to him that I could be a good mother for his child like his ex-wife was.

One of the pressures on their marriage was Janet's family's strong disapproval. By this time her parents had moved to the west coast.

My parents didn't believe in divorce. This was an embarrassment to them. Even after we were married, my mother refused to acknowledge the fact that I had a husband. I mean when I went out there for vacation, she would leave the room if I mentioned him, and if I called home to see how things were going I couldn't refer to him. That was a problem, and we had enough problems in the marriage with nobody giving any support in anything. My sisters were okay. They accepted it and stuff like that, but nobody helped.

Janet was happy when she became pregnant with Johnny. Nonetheless, she did not like all aspects of the pregancy.

I liked the fact that I was pregnant, but I looked ugly. Especially toward the end of the pregnancy, I felt real ugly. I think that I suffered more from the heat. The day he was born it was a hundred and five degrees. I could have suffered more; there was nothing about it that was really bad. Sometimes people would pat my stomach in the supermarket, and it was funny. I realized that there are some perverts who like pregnant ladies, who would reach right under my shift and then walk away. I was kind of upset. Kids love to touch it.

Ken was okay, I guess. He wasn't excited about it. I always figured it was because he had been through two pregnancies, so it wasn't as exciting to him. He was kind of a drag about it. He wouldn't take classes with me, and I expected him to. In the beginning it was pretty much his idea, and then it became a reality.

Delivery was easier than Janet had expected.

I expected worse because they had measured me and I expected to be put to sleep and wake up with stitches. By that point I had been convinced that that was what was going to happen. They told me when I was five months pregnant that it would probably be Cesarean. And so they allowed me three pushes, and it was after the third push. My mother is smaller than me and had nine kids, all naturally. You can sort of feel it; I knew when he was going to be born. If he didn't come on the third push I would have screamed because I could feel it.

I had a peridural. They work the same as Novocain and stuff. I guess it doesn't mean anything; I had a peridural but I felt it. Novocain has no effect on my mother and very little effect on any of the kids. There is a medical term for that. I could still walk. I got onto the delivery table myself.

Janet left the hospital after three days. Though her mother ignored the birth, a sister tried to provide some help.

My sister came. Of course, it really wasn't much help — it was a real drag. When my sister came she brought her nine-month- old kid, and there was too much happening at once. She was there for two days and I said, "Why don't you go away?"

I felt really tired. I guess I didn't go through any real depression except that I was tired because of waking up in the middle of the night. I was so tired with just the whole ordeal I just wanted to sleep and sleep and sleep. And I didn't have help. And I felt so guilty about that, too, because Ken offered help, but here he was working twelve hours a day. I couldn't see him getting up in the middle of the night to feed the baby or to help me do this and that, which is probably wrong because I was working a good twenty-four hours a day.

Ken's mother cared for the baby when Janet went back to work full time. Ken helped very little.

When Johnny was born I started saying, "Now wait a minute, you don't have two kids, you have three kids, and they all deserve your attention." That's what I thought. "I would never have done it if I didn't think you were going to devote as much time to him." But I was sadly mistaken, and finally I just think it became a problem. I resented the fact that he was giving her all this money. Looking back on it I should never have had... it's awful to say. I probably never would have had a better situation with him. It was going downhill. I sort of fooled myself into believing that once I had a baby things would get better; instead they got worse.

My idea was just totally different from what really happened. I expected him to help too, and he never so much as changed Johnny. He changed the baby's diapers twice in the whole time I had the baby.

But it all would be different if I had another kid, things would be a lot different. I would arrange things so that I wouldn't have to worry about getting a job a few days after I came home from the hospital, or money, or help. But with Johnny... all of a sudden, this is my kid! They just gave it to me, and I walked on to a life that is normal and yet I have a kid! I don't want it to be such a shock. The pregnancy was a shock; the baby was a bigger shock. It just like dropped into my lap. That's not my idea of having a kid. I think that I would have it be more of a sharing kind of thing. We would share it, everything.

Janet bottle-fed Johnny.

I couldn't breastfeed because I thought it wouldn't be fair to him or me, knowing that I was going to have to work before he was weaned. That's another thing that I would want to do, and I really missed out on that and I feel guilty, too. Sometimes I even lie when people ask me that question because you feel like you should have. A kid deserves that. This thing with the baby bottle scandal —how American marketing is killing off the babies in the Third World — I had thought about formula feeding my kid, and they promoted it to me. I just keep thinking about that. I stretched formula, not like they do or anywhere near it. I mean it was sterilized water, but I would stretch it a little. I'd get an extra bottle out of a can. But I was concerned with his nutrition, so I started making up for it and started serving him solid foods very early.

Although Janet worked, she was solely responsible for Johnny's care.

If we were home, it was me. He'd play with him when he came home. He'd change him if he peed — it was one of those things. He'd feed him. That was easier than changing him, I guess. But he did it. Johnny was weird when he was a little tiny baby. He'd suck so hard that he would choke himself, and it was really hard to feed him. I had to try him on different nipples. A couple of times he choked when Ken first start feeding him, and that really threw him. It threw me, too, but I knew he had to get fed. But I would just as soon not deal with Ken's anxiety. I'd do it myself.

In the beginning Janet found infant care very demanding and not very rewarding.

I liked him when he smiled. I liked him when he showed me that he was a human being. Once he grew out of the bundle of nerves and muscles I liked him. But I cannot say anything but that he was a drag before that. It took two months for me to really like him.

I didn't like the fact that he didn't know me but he was always crying and screaming for me to make him happy. So many times I did not know what was going to make him happy

— it would make me miserable and he would be miserable. And yet, I've seen it happen worse to other mothers. He was a relatively happy baby. He was a real good baby, and people always said that. It made me proud. I could understand the difference between a baby that wasn't good and a baby that was good. He was a great baby, but still he was a baby. He may not have cried a lot, and he grew, and he was healthy, but he was still a baby, and he was still there. There were still extra things to do.

Janet set out to prove that she was more capable than Ken's first wife.

I turned to nobody. My mother didn't talk to me anyway until he was two months old. I could see the difficulties Ken's wife had in raising their two children. She would flip over anything and everything. I wanted to show him that I was stronger than that. Of course, I always felt good that right next door to us was the fire department and that I could get him there if he choked before he had brain damage. I always felt in competition with the first wife.

Janet, who was experienced with infants, feels her difficulties were due to the heavy demands in other areas of her life.

I remember when I was in the hospital taking care of him and I put him on the bed and one of the husbands from the woman across the bed asked me if it was my first, and I was a little put off by that question. Did I look like I had twenty kids at home?... which I might have with the circles under my eyes. He said, "Because you handle him so well." We always took care of babies. My mother had babies left and right.

But her mother did not also work full time. Janet is acutely aware that her life is essentially different from her mother's. She was unprepared for and unhappy with the need to work full time throughout Johnny's early months and years.

My job as a female in life is different from my mother's. Her job was to be a mother and a housewife and to be happy doing that.

It would have been so much easier, I would have liked it so much better, if I knew I didn't have to work or worry about money. I know that that's a bad thing. It would have made things so much easier, I probably wouldn't have had any problems. I don't know what exactly would have come about, but it would have all worked out.

Janet worked throughout her pregnancy and continuously after Johnny was born. The family depended upon her income. For the first nine weeks postpartum she worked part time. After that she continued her part-time job and worked full time at the laundry.

I quit the laundry room; this is my biggest vacation. I'll never forget it. I quit the laundry room because I just couldn't deal with it, and I knew that in January — this was December — I was going to work full time at this store. I knew that this store that I'm in now was going to need me there. So I quit the laundry room and took three weeks off and that was like heaven, the longest time I'd ever taken off. And I spent three weeks being a mother, which is kind of bad, and then I started working in January.

Actually, Janet was still working her part-time job during those three weeks. It was the part-time position that she had held onto throughout her pregnancy and postpartum that finally expanded into the full-time position she likes.

But life with Ken continued to be problematic.

Ken went through a period of nine months of not working. Here I am working like a jerk being a mother, then he goes through this period for nine months of not working, going to see his kids all the time, not helping me out, not saying Johnny doesn't have to go to the grandmother's while he's not working. He gets in a motorcycle accident, and he's laid up for months, and I'm taking care of him. He was laid up for three months or two months or something like that. I mean where I had to lug this two hundred and ten pounds around to pee and to help him get dressed. Okay, he gets better. He's still limping and everything but he gets a job. I was upset he was not around anymore. I'm still working. We don't get to see each other that much anymore because he's working all these hours. Then I find out that he's involved with the waitresses. I just couldn't deal with that — I had taken enough. I followed him one day and banged on the door, and that was it. Since I was eighteen I had been devoting my whole life, all my energy, to making us work, and he did this to me. "Well, fuck it, buddy. This is where you're staying, now you're never coming home," I said. And everything's looked so much brighter since then.

When we spoke, Janet and Johnny lived with Steve. She worked four and a half days a week as manager of a gourmet food store, Tuesday through Saturday with Tuesday afternoon off to do her daycare turn. Steve worked six days a week, Monday through Saturday. Johnny was in cooperative daycare Monday through Friday. He spent Saturday, when daycare was closed, with his paternal grandmother. Johnny had just started daycare about six months earlier. Before that he spent all of Janet's work days with his grandmother. Janet was much happier now that he was in daycare

Because she's not the type of person I would like taking care of my kid. I feel I have to be fair to him; he loves his grandmother. She loves him, and one day a week I'd probably have to bring him by anyway to see her. But she just has so many ideas that are completely opposite of mine, and just that one day he's there makes such a difference in him.

She has real definite sexist ideas—that's the big thing. I mean a little boy should do this, little boys should do that. Only girls do this, only girls do that. My biggest example of it is, when he was two years old, he knew he had a penis, and he said to me, "Where's your penis?" And I kept saying, "I don't have one. I'm a lady. I'm a girl." And it didn't dawn on me till a while later that he couldn't figure out where mine went, so I just said I had a vagina. I didn't have to show him or anything. I just said it, and that answered the question. He knew that women had vaginas, men had penises. Well, when she found out — apparently he said to her, "You have a vagina"

— she was just appalled. It was fine for him to say penis but, to her, to come out and say vagina — I think she wanted to make up her cute little name for it. She actually said, "I think that's vulgar you taught him that. I think that he shouldn't learn that right now." And I said, "Well, you may think it's vulgar, but I don't, and I don't think there are many women my age who think it is anymore." Things like that really upset me. Plus, she sneaks him food I don't want him to eat, and she has all day long to spend catering to him where I don't have that, and so it's like Disneyland when he goes over there.

I feel more comfortable with what he learns at daycare. That's why I brought him there—because she had been taking care of him all the time.

Although Janet values Johnny's daycare, it does not solve all her childcare needs. She still must make many arrangements in order to work from ten to five-thirty.

I take Steve to work at seven-thirty, get myself and the baby ready, and lately a mother comes with her kid about eight-thirty, and I have these two little kids running around. I do it as a favor. I have to go anyway with one kid, so I might as well take two kids. I usually leave the house at quarter after nine, so I get to work early to get things ready. And that's a real nice part of my day, when I'm there and no one comes in. It's like the whole hassle of the morning — going to North Haven with Steve, going to daycare with the kids — I mean I resent that sometimes, not being able to get up, get dressed, and go to work like most people.

She works until five-thirty or six.

Daycare closes at five, which is a hassle. One of the other mothers, who has to go by me at work, drops him off at the shop. So that last half-hour is a real drag because that's when people usually rush into the store at the last minute.

Lately it's not so busy, and Steve has been getting a ride home with someone else. But sometimes I make the trip to North Haven, like I probably will today. We get home about six-thirty or quarter to seven. It's a really long day when you think about it. Just the work sounds like nothing.

When they get home Steve shares responsibility for house and child care.

> Steve is a lousy cook. He does all the dishes, so he also plays with the baby so I can do it. We eat around seven-thirty.

This is in keeping with their general sharing of responsibilities, and very different from her marriage with Ken.

> He does the dishwashing. When he comes home that's his thing to do. If he does it before he goes to work that's fine, but that's his job. I do light cleaning and straightening, only because he puts things where I get all screwed up trying to find them, and if I do it he knows where everything is. But he does heavy stuff. He does the floor washing, scrubbing down the bathroom, he does the garbage. It's funny because we joke about it, man's work and woman's work. It's like you take out the garbage because you're a man. And he's like, "You can carry out the garbage; you're as strong as me."

Her relationship with Steve is very different from her marriage to Ken in its expressiveness as well.

> After Johnny goes to bed we'll sit there, and I'll have a glass of wine, and he'll have a glass of beer, and we'll watch TV or talk. We do a lot of talking, and that's great. That's one thing I never did before. It is real nice, that time. We just talk about what we did during the day. Steve talks all the time to me. He doesn't really like his job so he'll talk about all of it to me. I don't even understand his job, but I listen. And I'll talk about frustrations with Johnny and stuff. He'll say, "Well, I'll do this in the future," or "We can't do this," or "We shouldn't do this." We talk about the future a lot because I have a tendency to blow up and not talk. I still do but I guess we both learned to accept that, and then I learned to accept his way of doing things. We try each evening to have some time to talk.

They also have Saturday nights to themselves.

Saturday is nice because Johnny, for the most part, will sleep over[at his grandmother's] Saturday night. I pick him up early Sunday morning and we have Saturday night, which most people really don't have — I really love it — to go out and eat or just hang around or do whatever you want to do. So it makes the week worthwhile to have that time to just unwind.

Sunday is nice because I go and pick up the baby while Steve cleans the kitchen and washes the floor. Then we come home and decide what we are going to do for the day. If Steve has something to do we go and do it, but for the most part it's "Let's do whatever you want to do." I've never had that. It's always been "This is what we are going to do." But now it's very much my decision, and it's so nice because we'll go somewhere the baby can enjoy, like the circus, or the aquarium in Mystic, and stuff. And that's just nice; it's nice to do. It was so nice yesterday: we were all together at my sister's house. Just the four sisters and all their kids. It was a big cook-out.

Steve does everything as much as I do, I think. It's completely different from when I was married and completely different from a lot of other situations I've seen. He gets up with Johnny in the morning. They have breakfast together. It's a toss up between who dresses him. We share everything: baths, etc. One person wants to get rid of him, they get rid of him.

Although Steve relates to Johnny like a parent, Ken is still his father.

Johnny knows him as a person in the background. Ken sees him, brings him things on birthdays and holidays and things. And he knows that he has to share him with the other two kids, who he really loves — his brothers. He loves them, looks up to them.

Ken sees Johnny infrequently.

When the divorce was finalized [about six months earlier] it was decided that he could see Johnny Monday at my residence, or any time he gave me twenty-four hours notice. I'm still waiting.

When he first left he would come regularly to see him, but it got to the point where he wasn't paying any attention to Johnny and he was just hassling me. I said it's uncomfortable, and I want you to wait for a while. Well, he started coming back again, and then he just didn't have the time anymore. He would call and say I don't have the time, after Johnny waited all morning for him to come, looking out the window. I couldn't put him through that anymore, or me, wasting a whole Monday morning waiting for him, wondering if he was coming or not. He has two other kids by a previous marriage, and with one day off a week, I guess he had to choose and he chose.

Ken does pay child support.

He pays it faithfully; ninety dollars a week. He never gave me anything beforehand, but he's got this job now where I know how much he's making so he's got to do it now. I paid my dues, and now I need help. Especially if this is what you want to do with your life, go from woman to woman and not face the responsibility of a child, of a wife, of somebody who cares for you and is working for you. You're going to have to start doing it now.

I opened a checking account as soon as I got enough money where you could actually open a checking account, where you don't feel embarrassed. He puts it in the checking account. He hasn't missed a payment except once at Christmastime I told him not to bother because I figured it was more important to me that he get Johnny something for Christmas. The day after Christmas he came to see Johnny.

With child support and both her and Steve's wages, finances are better than ever before. Their annual income is thirty-eight thousand dollars.

It's like heaven. I'm sure there are people who make more money and people who make less, but it is the first time in my life that I can say, "Gee, that's nice." My new couch — my first stick of furniture that hadn't been peed on. Of course my credit rating in still zilch because I haven't established it yet, and

Steve and I aren't married and stuff like that, but we are paying our rent.

He has the savings account, and I have the checking account. I pay the bills, and he puts some in the bank and gives me some every week. We split everything fifty-fifty. I put my check in the checking account. He gives me two hundred dollars for the checking account, and whatever else goes into the savings account, or we get something that we've been wanting. We trust each other. We talked about it because we were both really scared. We were going to get a car. Well, whose name does the car go in? But we already worked that out, an agreement between ourselves, that he'd have to pay me half. We'd split the money in the savings account if we split up.

About half of their income goes for joint expenses; the rest is each person's own.

We have to be careful because we have to live in a situation where we're roommates, not husband and wife. You see that's all in my mind, and everything has got to be split. If one person wants something then that's their expense. That couch is mine. I bought it out of my checking account money.

Janet keeps the accounts.

When I put my deposit in, I put my initials under it. When Ken deposits, I put Ken under it. And then I work it all out. It's very hard when Steve has a bill, and I have to send a check. It gets all screwed up like with the student loans because that comes out of his expenses. I have nothing to do with his student loans; I'll be damned if I'm going to pay for it. And his medical bills, my medical bills are all split. So when I write a check he's already given me the money for it. Sometimes we still get into little hassles over it, but we work them out. I show him all my records, and he shows me all his.

It's still hard for me to admit that I have plenty of money right now, because I'm always afraid that something is going to happen — it's going to be cut off. So we have to make sure we get it all in the bank.

Twenty-five and divorced for six months, Janet seems to have finally adjusted to motherhood.

This past year I think is when I got really used to having him around. It took me that long. It took me until he was in daycare, and I figured his situation was better and healthier. My situation got better and healthier for me, and I learned to just relax and accept the fact that he's here and we're together. And we're happy. But up until about a year ago, I still felt the newness of him and the shock of changing my life and the added responsibility. And I think a lot of it has to do with the fact that now, once he started daycare, I met a lot of other mothers with newer kids and talking to them I could reassure them about things. My sister had her baby when Johnny was almost two — this is the one who was married for six years before she had him — and it was like, "Jane, don't worry about it." I felt like the experienced mother, and in smoothing out other people's feelings or talking about them and realizing that they had the same feelings and sort of giving them a little more confidence, I gained more confidence. Even now, every day I think, "What am I doing?... I like it." I like having him, and I like knowing that I've overcome it, the big change. And now he's here. But I don't think I'd be willing to go through that again. I know it's going to be just as much of a shock to my system saying I have two kids as saying I have one. It's going to happen all over again. I don't know if I'm ready for it. I don't know if I'll ever be ready for it.

In spite of her serious misgivings, Janet does not rule out the idea of having another child someday; she just is not sure.

I probably will have another kid someday. Maybe my frame of mind will change. But right now I can't see it. It's hard enough working and taking care of things with one; I can't picture two. I probably will because I change. If in a couple of years I don't decide to have another one, then I'll have my tubes tied. I just don't want to be tied down to a kid for the rest of my life.

She feels that having a child has changed her. As difficult as the adjustment had been, it is hard for her to imagine being without him.

I'd miss him. If he wasn't around I'd go berserk. But yet there are times when I want him not to be around. I don't know how different it would be. I think I'd be lost without him. He's like my guiding light or something. As long as he's there, I have to be together. I don't think I'd go berserk or anything, but I think I'd be a lot less responsible. I'd want to go back to before I was married, when I was still single and carefree and took care of myself. I would want to do that, where I know I don't want to do it now. I want to take care of him.

She feels very committed to Johnny and is concerned that she not make the mistakes her parents made.

I think it's important that Johnny and I stay very close. I know there will be periods where we drift apart, but I want him to be able to accept me for what I am as I accept him for what he is. I know there's going to be conflicts there, there always is. Every parent wants their kids to communicate and be open with them and love them. I expect all those things but I also wouldn't have any fears about it not happening because I know there's going to be times when it does happen. I just want us always to like each other. I don't want him to grow up to be president of the United States; I just want him to be my kid.

I think a mistake parents make is expecting anything of them when they grow up, because the more you expect of them the more you're going to be thrown for a loop when they don't do what you expect. That's the problem my parents had and Steve's parents are having with their kids. I expect him just to be good, a good human being. Whatever he chooses to do in life that's up to him, and I hope I always can say that. And if he wants to go to college, I'm going to help him. If he doesn't, he'll have that money to do something else with.

Janet does not see her work life in fifteen years as very different from her present life, but she expects to be done with caring for little kids. She has neither career plans nor plans for more children.

> I expect I'd probably be doing the same basic thing, going to work every day. I would like to be doing something different; I'm not sure what exactly. I don't want to be having another baby or another little kid.

Janet was young and saw no other options when she decided to become a mother. She had only a high school education and no prospects of a career. Like most working-class girls, marriage and family were what she expected for herself. But in contrast to Linda, Janet's marriage brought hardship and pain, not happiness and financial security. The reality of Janet's marriage was that she had to work in spite of having a newborn. She struggled to adjust to motherhood, with little help from her husband or family. Three years after her baby's birth, divorced from his father, she finally feels happy about being a mother. Her mothering experience has made her more self-confident and more organized. And she plans never again to have a job and a baby at the same time.

10

Motherhood Today and Tomorrow

The preceding narratives show how becoming a mother changes women's lives. The birth of the first child, in Janet's words, "the big change," was a turning point for the women with whom I spoke. Having a child required them to dramatically change their daily activities. The physical exhaustion of pregnancy and childbirth, the constant demands of infant care, the emotional draw of the newborn—as well as the cultural expectation that mothering be full time—all call upon new mothers to focus attention on their family roles and to limit their other commitments, especially those that take them away from home.

Hearing these stories reminded me of the change that hit my life when I became a mother. As is so often the case, a minor event triggered a major shift in awareness. A few days after our first son was born, my husband went to a neighboring city to attend a conference. As involved as he was in the birth and care of our newborn, I suddenly realized that he could still leave to attend to public affairs, and I could not. While I could have gone to the meeting (if I had felt well enough), I certainly could not, would not have gone without the baby. Having a child had dramatically altered my life. This was a universal experience among the mothers I interviewed.

Nearly everyone altered her employment or schooling in response to her first pregnancy. One woman had never worked, so having a child did not affect her employment status, and three others continued working full time after their first child was born. But by the time their babies were born, everyone else either quit, took leaves of absence from work, stopped school, changed from full to part-time employment, or readjusted work schedules.[1] Some of the mothers left their jobs because they planned to devote themselves to raising a family. Others intended to continue their careers but altered their work pattern because they wanted to give their infants a good start. In either case, their lives were dramatically altered.

In spite of such similarities, the stories these women tell are varied. While mothering presents us all with similar demands, women have some control over how it gets incorporated into our lives. Some devoted themselves exclusively to mothering, others maintained their jobs. Some mothered singlehandedly, others with assistance from spouses, kin, or paid help. Some loved infant care, others merely tolerated it. But unlike their mates, they all did it.

Nor was the transition to motherhood equally difficult for all the women. Alice, Elizabeth, Linda, and Nina found the changes in their lives relatively easy to accommodate; Pam, Ellen, Amy, and Janet found adjustments considerably more difficult. The first group enjoyed life patterns during their early mothering years that were consistent with their expectations for work and family. Alice worked for two years after her child was born, but she knew it was short term, enjoyed her work, and was then able to become a full-time homemaker. Linda also had the resources to choose full-time homemaking. Elizabeth and Nina both wanted to continue their careers and, with the help of their husbands, were able to do so in addition to mothering.

By contrast, Ellen loved the idea of staying home but was less enamored of the reality of it. Janet wanted to be home with the baby, but working was an economic necessity. Amy and Pam stayed home as they felt they should, but wished they could have continued their careers. These women experienced conflicts between their needs to mother and their needs to work, making their early mothering years problematic.

Before their babies were born, about two-thirds of the mothers I interviewed expected to stay home as full-time mothers and homemakers. The others planned to continue employment.

Doing what she expected often eased the way through the transition to motherhood, but since the experience of new motherhood was somewhat of a shock, the new mother sometimes wished to alter her work plans. Unfortunately, financial necessity, family pressure, and childcare considerations frequently prevented changing employment status once the baby was born. This was the case for Janet. For Amy and Pam the internal pressures of wanting to be good mothers placed limits on their employment in spite of their career commitment. In Amy's case, the internal pressures were reinforced by family pressure, which seemed to intensify her conflict.

Each of these women was eager to talk about the major change of life that occurred when she became a mother. The extended interview was a helpful process for them, and for me as well. For a time, we became close. Most of the women had not spoken with anyone about their expectations and disappointments, their self-doubts and dissatisfactions with motherhood. The myth of motherhood as ultimate feminine fulfillment is so pervasive, so powerful, that it convinces each mother that her negative feelings must reflect her own inadequacy rather than problems shared by all mothers. Talking honestly helps to debunk the myth of maternal bliss and to see commonalities with other mothers. It also helps resolve concerns about being a less-than-perfect mother. For these reasons, the women found the interviews therapeutic. Some sent me notes in between sessions, or letters later on. Several asked me to come back to talk to a group of their friends. Many gave me names of friends who wanted to be interviewed.

For me, the joy was exploring my abstract questions about women's experiences through concrete autobiographies. While our contact lasted, I felt involved with each woman's concerns. She came to life; usually I met her children, and often her husband and other kin. But becoming intimate with many mothers enabled me to form impressions larger than any individual life.

Strategic Planning

One major theme emerged as I spoke to these women and learned about their choices and conflicts. The quality that most seemed to relate positively to adjustment and satisfaction was the extent of control a woman exerted over her life. I refer to this as "strategic planning." Strategic planning means looking toward the future with intent to shape it; doing those things that are possible to help achieve one's vision. Planning a pregnancy, saving money for a leave of absence, reducing work hours, lining up a babysitter, all are forms of strategic planning. Strategic planning implies perceiving options and making choices rather than simply drifting. As their stories reveal, these mothers differed greatly in how strategic they attempted to be.

Strategic planning was a quality that showed up in the lives of the career women again and again, so often that it appeared to represent nothing less than an approach to life. They prepared for careers, they planned the timing of their children, they prepared for childbirth, they arranged childcare help, they planned daily and weekly schedules to meet the needs of their families and their work.[2] While women without careers were sometimes organized, those with careers were characteristically so. Career women also held a different set of assumptions about the division of labor with their spouses. They were unlikely to assume that family responsibilities were solely their own and likely to establish shared, rather than traditional conjugal roles.

Career commitment was a characteristic developed by a quarter of these women early in life. Middle-class opportunities, higher educational attainment, and strong parental role models all contributed to the desire for a career. Most of the career women I interviewed were mobile and came from middle-class backgrounds. All attended college; most earned advanced degrees. Half were raised by very strong single parents who fulfilled the multiple roles required of parenting and employment. Another had for a father "a rare 'old country' person...[who] believed very firmly that the things you did made you happy, not just your love for somebody."

Career commitment was one of two reasons these women had for planning to combine motherhood and employment; the other was financial necessity. Since women are still often expected to give up employment when they become mothers and stay home to raise a family, continuing to work required an active decision. The plan to continue employment was typically formulated before conception or at the beginning of pregnancy.

Although their career commitment varied, none of the mothers with whom I spoke remembered giving serious consideration to remaining childless. Overall, only about five percent of all married women choose not to have children. All of these mothers saw having a child as a natural or desirable part of their lives.[3]

While all the women wanted to have children, what differed was the degree to which they planned their offspring. Quite a number started their families without an active decision. Four of ten first births were unplanned. In a small number of cases contraception failed, but in most it was not used. Couples either ignored the problem, or simply let nature take its course.[4] Linda called this being "free and easy; if I got pregnant, I got pregnant." For some, "free and easy" worked out pretty well. For others the consequences were surprising and dismaying. In their lives the pregnancies felt like accidents because, no matter how predictable they might have been, they were unplanned. Lack of planning did not necessarily imply that the babies were unwanted, just as planning did not insure complete fertility control. Planning did, however, imply a sense of self-determination on the woman's part that was reflected in many other areas of her life as well.

Six of ten mothers used contraception to control the timing of their first pregnancies. For them the decision was when, rather than whether to have a first child. Typically, a practical reason made the time seem right. Decisions rested on such considerations as age or career stage of themselves or their husbands. These concerns were often linked together. Many wanted time as a couple before a baby came along.[5] Reaching her late twenties, or just finishing a degree frequently triggered the wife's decision; sometimes the husband's greater age, or his having just finished school did. There were a variety of reasons, but all were practical.

Notably, all thirty mothers had used contraception to control their fertility for at least part of their married lives. The duration and rigor with which they used it, however, varied a great deal. For couples who began married life "free and easy," contraception or sterilization were options chosen only after one or more children were born. Other couples started out with plans to control their fertility, but failed to follow through because of the physical discomforts of the available contraceptive devices. A third group utilized contraception rigorously and effectively.

These styles of contraceptive use reflected a wide range of attitudes about family planning. On one end were the women like Elizabeth who took deliberate care with contraception and then, when their families were complete, had tubal ligations. On the other end were women like Linda, who used contraception less rigorously, had more children than planned, and still accepted that another accidental pregnancy might occur. Most women were between these two extremes. They used contraception effectively, but did not yet put a definite end to their childbearing. Or, although they planned reasonably well, they experienced an accidental pregnancy. Or they did not plan at all until they had enough children, then had their tubes tied, or their husbands had vasectomies. There are many scenarios for how a family grows: total planning, some planning, minimal planning.

Women with clear plans for continuing their careers while having their families were the ones who approached family planning in the most systematic fashion. Also systematic were the women who planned brief breaks or slow-downs in their careers while they had their children. Women who saw mothering as their job, or who had not formed plans about their lives outside of the family, were less strategic.

Education and relative prosperity fostered planning. Middle-class women with college educations were more likely to believe they could control their destinies. They learned in their families and in their educational experiences that they could be productive members of society as well as wives and mothers. They also had resources providing room for choice. They were likely to have professional and managerial husbands with good salaries, so they could choose to stay home and mother. Some had husbands with relatively flexible work schedules with whom they could share home responsibilities. If they worked, they were likely to be able to earn salaries good enough that they could expect to bring home more than they would have to pay for childcare and household help. But perhaps most importantly, they were likely to believe that they could be good mothers as well as teachers, editors, scientists, or whatever. They believed they could plan their lives so that neither family nor career would suffer. They believed their professional interests were legitimate. They believed in themselves.

Relationships with Spouses

Self-confidence enabled women with careers to form less traditional relationships with their mates. Because they wanted to continue their careers and because they generally resisted adopting feminine stereotypes, they did not simply assume they would or should be solely responsible for family maintenance. This led to sharing of roles, which in turn fostered closer conjugal relationships. None of the women with careers had a marriage with a completely traditional sex-role division of labor.[6] About half had husbands who shared child and household care. Like Elizabeth and Walter, each partner was primarily responsible for different household tasks or for childcare at different times, but they also did a lot of things together. The other half had husbands who helped; although the women were primarily responsible, when the men were home they did a substantial amount of family work. While it is generally true that husbands of employed wives help more at home than husbands of homemakers, some of these husbands of career women were actually doing close to their fair share.

In contrast, the women who were not oriented to careers had more traditional marriages and enjoyed substantially less help from their husbands. Only Janet, who was employed full time, had a mate who shared responsibility for home and child care. About seven in ten had mates who helped when they were around. Two in ten had mates who did not regularly participate in child or home care, which was a significant source of marital tension and bitterness.

While commitment to career on the part of the wife promoted the formation of a marriage with shared roles, a wife having a job also increased the involvement of the husband in childcare. Working even just a few hours each week necessitates a kind of planning that full-time mothering does not.[7] It requires childcare help which demands prior arrangements with other adults. The more hours of work, the more assistance required. Of the full-time employed workers, half used daycare centers, half had regular sitters. The women who worked part-time relied on their husbands, their housekeepers, nursery schools, and babysitters. Only one used daycare. All the employed mothers received some help from their mates as well.

While some marriages started out by design with spouses sharing both breadwinning and homemaking roles, others became more sharing as children added to the burdens of two working parents. Although there was sometimes conflict about the sharing of roles, typically the women felt closer to their mates as a result. They shared more common interests and had better communication. The most stereotypic division of labor occurred when the woman was a full-time homemaker without commitment to a career, living near extended family.

Local Kin

Being pregnant, anticipating childbirth, and having a newborn to care for are all new and weighty experiences. As they faced these responsibilities for the first time, the women looked to their loved ones for help and emotional support. They turned to their mothers and female kin as well as to their husbands.[8] Female kin, especially mothers, took on a new importance. First pregnancy brought most of the women emotionally closer to their mothers, even those who had previously felt estranged. Most spoke of a new connection between themselves and their mothers as they anticipated giving birth.[9] As a mother of a five-month-old put it, "I was always close to my mother, but now I really need her." Although I had already lived on my own for seven years, when my mother came for a week to help after

I brought my first-born home from the hospital I did not want her to ever leave.

Female kin who lived close by supplied generous amounts of practical and emotional support and had considerable impact on local women. This impact contained both positive and negative elements. Having mothers and other female kin at hand provided the woman with help and reassurance during the transition to motherhood; it also reinforced traditional family values which discouraged attending childbirth classes, breastfeeding, and role sharing with spouses. Local mothers encouraged their daughters to become mothers and homemakers, and furnished emotional and material support for adopting those roles in traditional ways. Offers of maternity clothes and cribs, companionship, and entry into the adult community of mothers served as enticements to maternity. This conservative social context influenced the local women to plan less, to accept motherhood as the next step in their lives and, therefore, to become pregnant sooner than their mobile counterparts. It also decreased the degree to which they called upon their husbands to participate in childbirth and infant care; if help was needed, kinswomen were ready and waiting to provide it.

While extended families almost always responded positively to the news of a new baby on the way and usually provided some help after the birth, local women received assistance more frequently and for longer duration than did mobile women. Although most of the women had outside help of one sort or another after they gave birth, a new mother living away from her kin was about twice as likely to be without outside assistance as her local counterpart. Whether new mothers were local or mobile, outside help most often came from kin; but for local women help from kin was less formal and less likely to suddenly come to an abrupt end. A mother living at a geographical distance had to plan a trip to come and help, while a local one could simply drop by for a few minutes, a few hours, or longer. For most mobile women like myself, help from kin lasted the duration of a postpartum visit, typically a week or two. For most local women help from kin continued indefinitely.[10]

Local women had networks of relations that provided a wide range of helpful services: childcare, shopping, sick care, food preparation, a ride or a car to borrow, companionship, as well as advice and know how. They frequently had friends of long standing who were part of their networks as well, "girls" with whom they had gone to school and whom they had known virtually all their lives. Moreover, local women were also likely to add in-laws to their social resources by marrying men from the local community.[11] Two-thirds of the local women were married to local men.

Mobility, in contrast, stretched the threads of women's family networks so severely that while some served in special but irregular ways, others broke altogether. One of ten mobile women were married to men with kin nearby; in those cases in-laws provided considerable help and financial support, and consequently exerted substantial influence on the daily life of the family. But in most cases there was limited extended family assistance. Parents and siblings were sometimes called on in an emergency, good friends often stayed in touch, but until new friends were made, there was no one to help on a day-to-day basis but one's husband, one's pediatrician, or paid help.[12] As a result, spouses played a larger role in helping mobile women — their participation was both more needed and more forthcoming.

Attitudes Toward Pregnancy and Childbirth

As I spoke with these women I began to see that while motherhood is important to all of them, they approach it with different attitudes and values. While some are trying to follow the traditional model of their mothers, others are seeking new approaches to mothering. Pregnancy, childbirth, and infant care are the initial stages of motherhood. By looking at them we can see the diversity of attitudes about what good mothering entails and how mobility affects these attitudes.

Women who held traditional views of women's role as mother and planned to stay home as full-time caretakers of their children enjoyed pregnancy more and felt less conflicted about it.[13] Higher educational attainment, greater career commitment, and a greater desire to combine employment and motherhood all require resisting the cultural stereotype of the at-home mother. While such resistance helps women shape their lives and positively affects every other aspect of motherhood, the disadvantage is that it makes pregnancy more conflictual, in spite of the active desire for a child. In contrast, local extended-family encouragement, attention, and support help make pregnancy a strongly positive experience but negatively affect other aspects of mothering.

Among them, these thirty mothers had experienced seventy successful pregnancies. Their stories reveal the tremendous physical effort that is an essential aspect of pregnancy.[14] Everyone remembers experiencing rapid body changes, being tired, having occasional muscle spasms or backaches, feeling that the last month or two would last forever. These are the normal physical demands of pregnancy.[15] As a thirty-seven-year-old mother of a fourteen-month-old, considering the timing of her next pregnancy, put it, "Being pregnant is a lot of work." One-quarter of the mothers had only routine physical complaints. The remaining three-quarters had other complaints as well. Nausea was the most frequently mentioned physical discomfort of pregnancy; half of the women I interviewed suffered from it. The second most frequent physical complaint was size — being big, clumsy, heavy. Less frequent, but often more serious complaints were edema, toxemia, varicose veins, phlebitis, toxoplasmosis, and Rh incompatibility. Often several of these discomforts occurred in the same pregnancy.

Physical demands and discomforts, essential though they are, create only some of the difficulties of pregnancy. The stories also reveal the psychological effort required by pregnancy, especially for women with careers that they value. Pregnancy is a transition from a relatively independent existence to life with a new, dependent child. As such it requires psychological, as well as physical, growth and change. It is a developmental stage characterized by psychological activity and emotional disequilibrium.[16] Again and again I heard stories about how being pregnant made the women feel vulnerable because they were big and clumsy, or anxious about what lay ahead, or more dependent upon their husbands and their obstetricians. I also heard how it restricted personal freedom because responsibility to an unborn child required treating their bodies more carefully than usual. This included not eating junk food, not smoking, not drinking alcohol or coffee, and not taking aspirin for a headache. Feelings of guilt sometimes contributed to the psychological disequilibrium. Accidental pregnancies often brought dismay, at least at first, wishes for miscarriages, even thoughts of abortion.[17]

In spite of the physical and emotional demands, pregnancy was a strongly positive experience for some of the mothers. Most of the women, in fact, were enchanted with the experience of their first pregnancy, then felt more matter-of-fact, even negative, about subsequent ones.[18] Later pregnancies usually entailed more physical discomforts in the form of fatigue, backaches, larger girth sooner, and more weight. In addition, with at least one child already, the mother-to-be could not set her own pace.

A minority of the mothers, all mobile women who were committed to careers, describe even the first pregnancy as a matter-of-fact experience. It was the way to get babies, so they were willing to put up with it. Five of the women, including Elizabeth, Pam, and Nina, felt this way — happy to be having a child but not thrilled with the process. These five women had a great deal in common. They all had intact first marriages. They each had successfully planned all of their pregnancies. They all had careers that were important to them and had been employed almost continuously since having children. In addition, they were women who were mobile when they had children.[19] None of them had a mother, or mother-in-law, in close proximity to emotionally support her through a pregnancy, or to admonish her for being committed to her career.[20] None of the twenty-five other women shared this pattern of characteristics. While the other women devoted themselves either to "family only" or "family first," these women put neither career nor family first; they refused to choose.[21]

The increased physical and psychological vulnerability of pregnancy sometimes threatened the self-image women with careers had of being in control of their lives, which led to the development of negative or ambivalent feelings. They resisted being swept away by traditional images and expectations of pregnancy; they preferred to be recognized for their professional accomplishments rather than simply for being pregnant. Yet they lacked positive images and models for being pregnant professionals. Most (all but Amy) had husbands who supported their plan to work as well as to mother. These characteristics made the pregnancy experience less positive, but favorably affected the birth and mothering experiences.

The local mothers-to-be felt more relaxed about their pregnancies and avoided thinking about the deliveries. They were less upset by their feelings of dependence or the tendency of others to infantalize them. Again, their relatives reinforced traditional attitudes about pregnancy, childbirth, and the division of labor. The pregnant women enjoyed the family attention and excitement, learned from female kin what to expect, and did not seek formal preparation for childbirth and infant care. Only a third of the local women prepared for childbirth by taking classes with their husbands.

Mobile women typically felt less at ease with their pregnancies, had fewer sources of informal information, and sought more formal preparation for childbirth and childcare by attending classes. Preparing for childbirth is a way of establishing control in an anxiety-producing situation. It creates the conditions for a better birth experience. Women who attended classes were more self-assured and less afraid during delivery, and had better-informed husbands with them to serve as their allies against impersonal treatment by hospital staff. Two-thirds of the mobile women who gave birth took classes with their husbands.

Preparation for Childbirth

Preparation for childbirth, again a form of strategic planning, had a far-reaching positive impact on the transition to motherhood. Women who attended childbirth classes were more likely to have their husbands with them for delivery. Medication was lighter when husbands were present than when the women were alone. Thirty-seven percent of the births attended by husbands were without anesthetic; only eighteen percent of the others were drug-free. In more than a third of the unaccompanied deliveries, drugs rendered the woman unconscious. This never occurred if the husband was present.[22] This finding is consistent with research that has shown that having a supportive partner at the laboring woman's side contributes to a positive labor and delivery experience. Women who interact more with their partners during labor express less pain and tension.[23] Having a supportive partner with the laboring woman throughout delivery reduces the length of time in labor and the need for surgical intervention.[24] Perhaps knowing the partner will remain throughout delivery increases, or prolongs, the analgesic effect. In addition to having less medication, the mothers enjoyed their deliveries more when their mates were with them. Being together for this momentous event made the women feel closer to their husbands. These positive birth experiences form an essential part of the new mother's adjustment to motherhood and her enjoyment of the new child.[25]

Being prepared for childbirth made it more likely that the woman would be conscious for her first delivery; only one of the fifteen women who took classes had gas during her first delivery, while more than a third of the women who did not take classes were given gas. Preparation also made it less likely that any anesthetic would be used during the first delivery; one-third of the women who took classes and had vaginal deliveries had natural childbirth, while none of the other women did. Preparation also made it more likely that the partner would be present at the first delivery; more than half of the women who were prepared and had vaginal deliveries had their mates with them, while less than a quarter of the other women who had vaginal deliveries did.

Since childbirth classes seemed important in establishing control and paternal involvement at an early stage of motherhood, I examined whether occupational background or mobility were involved with this choice. The occupational background of the women was not related to attendance at these classes. More than half of the women who attended classes came from working-class backgrounds; nearly eight in ten of those who did not attend came from middle-class backgrounds.[26] Living near kin, however, did seem to encourage women to reject the option of classes. Because they were less prepared, local women were less likely to have their husbands with them during their first birth (one-quarter of local, as opposed to nearly half of mobile husbands, were present for the first delivery).

Participation of Fathers

Furthermore, fathers involved in pregnancy and delivery were more likely to regularly participate in infant care. While nearly all of the fathers played with their babies regularly, the one in ten who did not were among the fathers not present at the delivery of any of their children.[27] Two-thirds of the fathers changed their babies routinely or often. Most of these were among the twenty-one fathers present for at least one of the deliveries of their children. Very few of the fathers regularly bathed their infants; those who did had been present at delivery. Half of the fathers put their infants to bed on a regular basis. Again, nearly all of these had been present at delivery. Only two in ten of the fathers regularly took their infants out without their wives. All of these fathers had been present at delivery.

The participation of these thirty fathers in routine infant care varied greatly. Only a few did all of the routine tasks on a regular basis; only a few did none of the routine tasks on a regular basis. More than eighty percent regularly did some, but not all, of the routine tasks. Regular participation did not mean the father assumed primary or shared responsibility for childcare; it meant that the mother had help. According to the mothers, half of the fathers provided regular help with infant care when they were home, but did not rearrange their work lives to be home more.[28] As one mother put it, "I could count on him doing anything, only he wasn't with them that often." In only one of the thirty families, Nina's, did the father take an extended period of time off from work (a year and a half) to care for his infant. There was, in contrast, very little variability among the mothers. All mothers did all infant care tasks; what varied was how much help they had.

Once again we see the far-reaching importance of planning. In this case, preparation for childbirth contributes to the active involvement of the father. The father-to-be learns with his wife how to do some of the basic infant-care tasks and is therefore less scared of the newborn. He also feels closer to his wife and baby as a result of being an active partner during labor and, often, delivery. As one mother of four said of her husband, "He was allowed in the delivery room the last time and I think he wishes that he had seen all of them. He has a special feeling for her."

Attitudes About Breastfeeding

As with preparation for childbirth, attitudes about mothering affected the decision of whether or not to breastfeed. Again in keeping with traditional values, only one local mother nursed her first child for at least three months, while two- thirds of the mobile women did. In the case of nursing, class background and mobility were both factors. Only one of the mothers from a working-class family nursed her first child, and she was mobile. More than six in ten with middle-class backgrounds nursed their first child; three-quarters of those who did not were local. Women from middle-class backgrounds were much more likely to nurse than were those from working-class backgrounds, especially if they did not live near kin.[29]

While breastfeeding is not essential to raising a healthy baby or establishing a good mother-child relationship, it does promote both of these goals. Human milk is perfectly balanced for the nutritional needs of human infants and provides many immunities as well, thus contributing to the physical well-being of the infant. Breastfeeding requires that the infant be held in a good position for eye contact with its mother and that mother and baby be in frequent close interaction, thereby contributing to the psychological well-being of infant and mother.[30] Also, because they are so obviously key persons in fulfilling their babies' needs, breastfeeding mothers have more positive self-images as mothers than bottle-feeding ones.[31]

The mothers who breastfed did so because they considered it healthy and natural, because it was easier than having to prepare and warm bottles, and because they liked it. As one thirty-year-old mother of two put it, "It's one of the big pay-offs of being a woman."

The women who bottle-fed did so primarily for social reasons. Lack of emotional support for breastfeeding was mentioned most often. More than a third of the women who did not nurse their first child felt that they were either not encouraged to, or were actively discouraged from, nursing. In some instances the husband opposed it, in some the mother or mother-in-law opposed it. Inconvenience was the second most often mentioned reason. One mother just believed the bottle was easier; another felt nursing would have interfered with her active social life. One woman did not nurse because she knew she had to get back to work. The third most frequent reason for not nursing was that the baby was not getting enough food. About two in ten mothers said this was why they did not nurse, although each felt somewhat relieved by that outcome.[32] A fourth reason mentioned was modesty.

Jan, a part-time college student at age forty-four, gave birth to her third child in a new marriage when her first two children were thirteen and twelve. Her two different sets of feelings about breastfeeding expressed the sentiments of both those who chose it and those who did not.

> I nursed Davey, which I did not the other two boys. I had very different feelings about that, a better feeling about my body as a woman — not that my breasts were some sort of sex objects. I remember thinking about nursing with the other two and not wanting to be a cow. With Davey it was just like I was the primitive woman out in the field. It was such a marvelous feeling—one of the best experiences I have ever had.

About four in ten of the mothers breastfed their first baby for at least three months; two in ten tried breastfeeding, though they did not succeed or persist; and four in ten did not even try.[33] Two-thirds of the successful nursers were women who had gone to childbirth classes with their husbands before delivery, while only one-third had not attended classes. Half of the women who prepared for childbirth nursed successfully, while less than a third of the women who did not prepare nursed successfully.[34] Classes promote breastfeeding by informing parents-to-be of its health benefits to the infant, as well as by giving it social endorsement. This enables both partners to accept the idea before the birth and to be supportive of each other in the face of negative family pressure.

Being mobile, attending childbirth classes, and having middle-class backgrounds were all related to successful breastfeeding. These factors seem to work together to promote feeling comfortable with one's body and to encourage questioning of traditional values. It is important to note that these same factors were also related to career commitment.

Patterns of Mobility and Planning

Several patterns emerge from these findings. First, local and mobile women entered into motherhood differently. Local women became pregnant sooner and with less planning. They received more family support for pregnancy as well as more postpartum help from female kin. In contrast, mobile women typically planned the timing of their pregnancies more carefully. They were also more likely to be without help from family during pregnancy and without help or with time-limited help from kin during the postpartum period.

Second, pregnancy, childbirth, and postpartum, all important features of the transition to motherhood, seem to be affected in different ways by the attitudes of the mother-to-be. Pregnancy — especially first pregnancy — seems to be enjoyed more by women who see family as their only, or their primary, commitment. This is probably because their view of pregnancy is culturally sanctioned. Women who are equally committed to their careers find pregnancy an ambivalently joyous, more matter-of-fact experience. Furthermore, women who plan ahead and approach childbirth by taking classes find the experience less frightening and more pleasurable than women who approach childbirth passively. Here, of course, women with commitment to careers are among those who plan, while the home-oriented women often do not.

Third, these findings refute the notion that mothers are either career-oriented or family-oriented. The career-oriented women were no less family-oriented than the full-time home-makers. They valued other commitments, particularly their work, but they valued their families and family life no less as a result. There are, of course, career-oriented women who choose not to have children, but they are not mothers and, therefore, were not a part of this study. These mothers, whether career-oriented or not, were family-oriented. All maintained a commitment to being good mothers, though they differed in some of their ideas about what good mothering entailed. For some it meant breastfeeding, for others it did not. For some it meant being full-time caretaker of the children; for others it included good alternate care. All the mothers, in fact, used alternate care for their children some of the time, but employed career women used it more regularly and, perhaps because of that, were often more careful about its selection.[35]

All mothers needed to spend time with their children and away from their children. Though employed mothers were not with their children all the time, they devoted almost all of their non-working hours to their children. Their recreation typically included the entire family. They felt less need to get away from the kids to relax than was expressed by the full-time homemakers who more regularly went out in the evening with their husbands or with "the girls." Full-time homemakers were not always home with the kids during the day, either. Husbands, mothers, sisters, and/or sitters provided some childcare relief, often at regular times each week. Even Linda, who felt so strongly that mothers should be home, had her "day off" each week.

Satisfaction with Motherhood

The transition to motherhood, important though it is, is only a small portion of the mothering years. Motherhood, once begun, never ends, although the level and type of demands change. Two of the women in this study had been mothers for only a couple of years, while others had been for nearly twenty years. How had motherhood affected their lives? At the conclusion of the interviews I asked each woman that question.

While nearly all of the women found motherhood much more demanding than they had anticipated, this was especially true for the at-home mothers. The words of one thirty-eight-year-old mother of two, who receives no home or childcare help from her husband, reveal the distress full-time homemakers frequently expressed.

> Sometimes I just feel like everybody is sucking from me — nothing is left of me, nothing to give, I'm just being drained. It's a lot harder than I ever realized. I thought it would be very easy. It's really very hard—much more responsibility than I ever dreamed of. Sometimes I just want to get away from it all, just go off and forget it. But you can't.

Women with careers or jobs did "get away from it all," not in the sense that Molly meant but in the regular way that going off to work insures. This provided them with some perspective on family problems and additional avenues of self-esteem and personal gratification. The same was true for homemakers like Alice who chose not to pursue a career but did seriously participate in community organizations.

The women with career commitment were overwhelmingly positive about the impact of being a mother on their own development. They felt that as a consequence they knew themselves better; that it made them more organized; that it brought them closer to their mates; that it brought them the family they never had growing up. The home-oriented women were largely positive, but more than a third of their responses were negative. They said that it made them less egocentric: they learned to plan for the kids, not themselves; that it brought enjoyment; that it made them see what life was really like; that it brought a new depth of caring; that it enabled them to know themselves better; that it took away their individuality by arresting intellectual development or making them dependent; that it was stressful; and it did not leave enough time for them to spend with their mates.

Overall, the major impact of mothering was positive. The women felt that they grew, they learned, they became more sensitive and loving. They also got a lot of pleasure from their children. For women who were devoting themselves exclusively to their families, this was sometimes accompanied by a feeling of having lost a part of their individuality. As one forty-one- year-old mother of six expressed it, "I put my own talents in the icebox for twenty years."

These women all had young children so many years lay ahead of them, first with their children and then without. Most had some vision of what she would be doing in fifteen years, when her youngest would be in college or, at least, high school. Two-thirds of the career-oriented mothers had specific plans for the future; the others had vague plans. Of the mothers without career-orientation, about twenty percent had specific plans, sixty percent had vague plans, and twenty percent had no plans. One in ten expressed fear about the future. Having either career commitment or a job made imagining the future without young children easier, in many cases exciting. More than half of the career-oriented or employed women cherished specific plans to which they looked forward. The rest entertained vague plans. Not even twenty percent of the homemakers without career commitment conceptualized specific plans for the future. A quarter had no plans; they doubted they could be anything besides caretakers.

Looking To The Future

Although these interviews involved only thirty mothers, I have spoken less formally with many other women as well. In addition to talking with women I know, I have given talks about my research and about the problems of combining employment and motherhood at public libraries, to audiences comprised mostly of mothers and mothers-to-be. I have listened to their experiences, their frustrations, their joys. As a college professor I have talked to many college-age women about their hopes, dreams, and fears for the future. It seems that more college-educated women, though certainly not all, are oriented toward careers than in the past. Most, however, are also committed to being wives and mothers.

The problems of employment, career, and motherhood reflected in the lives of the women in this book are the problems that I hear women discussing again and again. A growing proportion of young women are and will be facing the conflicts between their labor force and their family commitments. As more women attend college, as the expectation that women should work increases, as fewer men earn enough to support a family in middle-class style, and as the divorce rate remains high, it becomes increasingly irrational, and perhaps foolhardy, to expect women to become full-time homemakers when they become mothers.

As these women's varied stories demonstrate, there is no single way to arrange work and motherhood that is right for all women. Different women enjoy different choices and different choices have different pressures. Strategic planning, however, seems to provide the key to increasing life satisfaction and reducing stress. Women who become full-time homemakers because the job fits their skills and desires are happier and healthier than women who become full-time homemakers out of a sense of feminine duty. Employed mothers who choose to work, and choose their work, are happier than those who are forced to work at jobs that are demanding but give them little control.[36] Women do best when they consider the role of full-time mother and homemaker as they would consider any job, rather than assume it is their fate. This means weighing the alternatives. It also means discussing the terms of homemaking with their mates, rather than taking on all associated tasks singlehandedly.

Whether a woman chooses to continue employment or to be at home full time, planning is beneficial. If she lives near kin she should resist the added temptation to simply drift into motherhood and homemaking. Childbirth classes, active involvement of fathers, and provisions for breaks from constant childcare responsibilities all make mothering more enjoyable and less stressful, even for the at-home mother. Likewise, planning for life after active mothering makes the future appear exciting rather than frightening.

Social values are changing in ways that facilitate choice. More young women are learning to value the place of work in their lives. More young men are seeking wives who have professions. But the problems for women combining career and family have not been solved. More support services for parents of young children are needed. Nonprofit, neighborhood and work-based childcare centers, flex-time work schedules, and reliable afterschool programs are a few solutions that have been implemented in some places. Many individual women and couples have forged ahead and have created their own alternatives. They split shifts, or job share, or find good daycare, or form cooperatives with other couples like themselves. For the most part, however, women continue to bear the burden of rearing their children, because as individuals they lack the organization skills or resources to challenge the traditional expectations of full-time, at-home mothering. In many cases they have no mate and must go it alone.

While I do not believe that these problems of employment and motherhood should be the sole responsibility of women, or can be solved individually, the fact is that women are facing these problems and some women are able to handle them better than others. What researching and writing this book has taught me is the importance of strategic planning in the lives of women. While women cannot do everything, with planning, with support and help from their partners, and with some luck, they can do a lot and benefit as a result. Educating ourselves and our daughters to seek information, to consider all our options, and to make forward-looking choices can maximize our ability to pursue family and career commitments and enjoy the joint benefits they provide. Educating our husbands and sons to share responsibility for family work can help as well.

Appendix
About the Study

The material for this book is based on interviews with thirty white, middle-class mothers from southern Connecticut. Limiting my sample in number, race, class, and geography precluded it from being representative of all mothers, but enabled me to do in-depth work with a segment of the population that I was in the best position to understand because I belong to it. I limited my interviewing area to enable me to get from house-to-house efficiently, and also to insure that the social services available to the mothers were essentially the same: if one used babysitters or daycare and another did not it was not as a result of differential availability.

I used what is called the "snowball" method to select my sample. My initial contact with a woman was always through a mutual acquaintance. A colleague or a nursery school teacher would tell a mother about my project and ask if I could call. Then I would telephone, explain what I was doing, answer questions, and make an appointment. The women I interviewed gave me names of friends, relatives, and neighbors in this same manner. They enjoyed the opportunity to talk about themselves and felt other women would as well.

In the interviews I asked about many aspects of the woman's life: her childhood experiences and expectations, early family relationships, academic and work histories, courtship and marriage experiences, the decision to have children, conjugal relationship and division of labor, pregnancy and childbirth experiences, childrearing attitudes and experiences, friendship networks, and expectations for the future. I used a semistructured interviewing method, making sure to cover all the topic areas I wanted to learn about, but I did so by adjusting the order and wording of the questions to the flow of the conversation. This allowed a woman to follow her own train of thought, as well as to talk about things I did not anticipate.

All the interviews were taped and later transcribed. A research assistant and I listened to each of the tapes and independently coded some of the women's responses in order to establish reliable quantitative measures. For the most part, however, I was interested in the rich qualitative nature of the material, which I worked with using the transcripts and occasionally the tapes.

I selected women with preschool children, without considering their marital status. Nonetheless, every woman that I interviewed was living with a man. Twenty-four of the thirty lived with their first husbands. Five were remarried and lived with their second husbands, or, in one case, her third husband. One was divorced and lived with a man who was also divorced.

The women ranged from 22 to 44 years of age. Their mean age was 33.5 years. Their average number of children was 2.5. Thirteen of the women had two children. Six had one, and six had three. Two had five, and one had six. Most, but not all of the children were living at home; a few were away at college or on their own.

While all of the women considered their current families to be middle class, there were considerable differences in their levels of income.[1] The lowest reported income was $16,500 per year for a family of four; the highest $82,000 for a family of seven.[2] Six of the families earned under $28,000, the regional average annual pay.[3] Sixteen earned between $28,000 and $48,000, and eight over $48,000. While income level reflects class, occupation is the single best indicator.[4] With women, however, looking at occupation is problematic, especially during the childbearing years. To determine her class, therefore, I used a combined measure of the woman's educational level, her husband's educational level, and his occupation.[5] I considered a woman working class if she had no more than a high school education, and was married to a man with a similar educational background whose occupation was blue collar. I considered a woman middle class if she had at least a college education, and was married to a man with a similar educational background whose occupation was professional or managerial. When a woman did not neatly fit into one of the categories I made a judgement based upon the other information that I had. The composition of the group, by this measure, was three from the working class, twelve from the lower-middle class, and fifteen from the upper-middle class.

Based upon the occupations of their fathers, twelve of the women came from working-class, and eighteen from middle-class backgrounds.[6] The women with middle-class backgrounds spent, on average, six months more on their own before marrying than did those from working-class backgrounds (2.9 versus 2.4 years). They married, however, two years earlier, on average, than the working-class women (22.2 versus 24.2 years). They accomplished the combination of longer time on their own and earlier marriage by leaving their parents' home sooner, at the average age of 20.2, in contrast to 21.0 years for those from working-class families of origin.

All of the women had completed high school and all but four had attended some college. At the time of the interviews ten had only a high school diploma, two had associate's degrees, seven had bachelor's degrees, nine had master's degrees, and two had doctorates. Several still intended to complete college; one, in fact, was a part-time student.

Eight of the women in this study were oriented toward careers; they were committed to continuing their careers after starting their families. They had three different visions of how they would do this. Two, a college professor and an elementary school teacher, planned to continue to work full time, perhaps with a modification of schedule. One, a research scientist, planned full-time work except for a year off for full-time mothering after the birth of each child. Five planned to continue employment on a part-time basis while their children were young, after which they expected to return full time.[7] One was an editor, one a writer, one a social worker, and two were teachers.

When I spoke with them, only five of the women clearly fit into the category "full-time employed." By comparison, of the thirty men living with these women, twenty-nine clearly fit this category (the other was a writer and worked at home). Another ten of the thirty women worked part time. Six had part-time responsibilities at regular times each week. The remaining four part-time employed women had hours that varied from week to week.

Twelve of the women were "local": they lived within fifteen minutes driving distance from the place where they were raised, near parents and/or some siblings. Eighteen were "mobile": they had moved away from their kin and community of orientation and lived with their husbands in a new location.[8]

The mobile women married later than local women (at a mean of 24.0 years old compared to 21.6 years) and spent more time living on their own before marriage (3.3 compared to 1.8 years). Most went to college, some to graduate school, some worked. Local women, on the other hand, spent more of their early adult years working, less in school. Five women in each group had only a high school diploma (42 percent of the local, 28 percent of the mobile women), but the mobile women held many more advanced degrees. In comparison to the local women, the typical mobile woman had spent more than two additional years in school (16.7 years compared to 14.5).

Only three of the eighteen mobile women moved directly from the home of their parents to their married home. In contrast, many local women lived at home during early adulthood; five of the twelve never lived on their own before marriage. Of the eight local women who attended college, five attended colleges within ten miles of home, two went to a junior college an hour away, and only one went away, living in several different locations before finally settling back in her local area.

The local women are, on average, five years younger than the mobile women (30.5 years, compared to 35.7), although they have the same average number of children (2.5 children for local, 2.4 for mobile). Local women gave birth to their first child thirteen months sooner on average than their mobile counterparts (24.8 versus 25.9 years). They also had nearly twice the number of unplanned pregnancies, an average of 1.25 compared to .67 for mobile women.

Notes

Chapter One: Changing Ideas About Motherhood

1. Barbara Harris, "Careers, Conflict, and Children: The Legacy of the Cult of Domesticity," in Alan Roland and Barbara Harris, eds., *Career and Motherhood: Struggles for a New Identity* (New York: Human Sciences Press, 1979), 71.

2. See John Mack Faragher, *Women and Men on the Overland Trail* (New Haven, Conn.: Yale University Press, 1979), chapter 2, for a detailed description of the division of labor between the sexes in subsistence farm families of the Midwest.

3. Phillipe Aries, in *Centuries of Childhood* (New York: Knopf, 1962), has pointed out that childhood itself is a relatively recent invention.

4. Eli Zaretsky, *Capitalism, the Family, and Personal Life* (New York: Harper Colophon, 1976).

5. Bernice Lott, *Becoming a Woman* (Springfield, Ill.: Charles C. Thomas, 1981), 206. James Mohr, in *Abortion in America* (New York: Oxford, 1978), Chapter 4, points out that from 1840-80 abortion was widely used by native-born women to limit family size.

6. Judith Guss Teicholz, "Psychological Correlates of Voluntary Childlessness in Married Women," (paper presented to the Eastern Psychological Association, Washington, D.C., Mar. 1978), reports that, although fertility rates have decreased, statistics do not indicate an increase in the number of married couples that have chosen to remain childless. Throughout the twentieth century a constant 5 percent of the married population has chosen childlessness. In 1988 5.4% of wives expected to have no children. U.S. Bureau of the Census, *Statistical Abstract of the United States: 1990*, 110th ed., (Washington, D.C., 1990), 70. Surveys of women students in my classes over the years consistently indicate that about 80% want to have two children. In 1988 the average number of children expected by currently

married women was 2.2. National Center for Health Statistics. *Health, United States, 1989.* (Hyattsville, Maryland: Public Health Service, 1990), 95.

7. Robert Wells, "Women's Lives Transformed: Demographic and Family Patterns in America, 1600-1970," in Carol Ruth Berkin and Mary Beth Norton, eds., *Women of America: A History* (Boston: Houghton Mifflin, 1979), 18.

8. In 1960 the fertility rate per 1,000 women ages 14-44 was 118.0 children; in 1970, it was 87.9; in 1980, it was 68.4; in 1988, it was 67.2. See National Center for Health Statistics, *Vital Statistics of the United States, 1988,* Vol. 1, Natality. DHHS Pub. No. (PHS) 89-1100, Public Health Service, (Washington: U.S. Government Printing Office, 1988, 1.

9. *Employment in Perspective: Working Women* (Washington, D.C.: U.S. Department of Labor, Bureau of Labor Statistics, 1980) Report 643; Janet L. Norwood & Elizabeth Waldman, *Women in the Labor Force: Some New Data Series* (Washington, D.C.: U.S. Department of Labor, Bureau of Labor Statistics, 1979) Report 575; and *20 Facts on Women Workers* (Washington, D.C.: U.S. Department of Labor, Office of the Secretary, Women's Bureau, 1980).

10. Valerie Kincade Oppenheimer, *The Female Labor Force in the United States: Demographic and Economic Factors Governing Its Growth and Changing Composition* (Westport, Ct.: Greenwood Press, 1970), chapter 1.

11. Jennifer Watson, *Women, Work and the Future: Workforce 2000* (Washington, D.C.: National Commission on Working Women of Wider Opportunities for Women, January, 1989).

12. A great deal has been written about the social pressure on girls and women that pushes them towards motherhood. See, for example, Jessie Bernard, *The Future of Motherhood* (New York: Penguin, 1974); Ellen Peck and Judith Senderowitz, eds., *Pronatalism: The Myth of Mom and Apple Pie* (New York: Thomas Y. Crowell, Co., 1974); and Jean E. Veevers, *Childless by Choice* (Toronto: Butterworth, 1980).

13. Matina Horner, "Femininity and Successful Achievement: A Basic Inconsistency," in Michele Hoffnung Garskof, ed., *Roles Women Play* (Monterey, Calif.: Brooks/Cole, 1971), 98.

Although Horner's empirical work has not been successfully replicated, her descriptions of the problems for women are still apt.

14. Janet Dreyfus Gray, in "The Married Professional Woman: An Examination of Her Role Conflicts and Coping Strategies," *Psychology of Women Quarterly*, 1983, 7, 235-43, points out that this is a less effective coping strategy among married professional women.

15. Helena Znaniecki Lopata, *Occupation Housewife* (New York: Oxford University Press, 1971), 200. Lopata's extensive interviews with Chicago area women led her to conclude that the birth of a first child is the "event causing the greatest discontinuity of personality in American middle-class women," especially if the birth is not followed by full-time involvement outside the home.

16. Carol Gilligan, Janie Victoria Ward, & Jill McLean Taylor, eds., *Mapping the Moral Domain* (Cambridge, Mass.: Harvard University Press, 1988).

17. Louise Kapp Howe, "The World of Women's Work," in Jeffrey P. Rosenfeld, (ed.), *Relationships: The Marriage and Family Reader* (Glenview, Illinois: Scott, Foresman and Co., 1982), 216-7.

18. Kathleen Gerson, *Hard Choices: How Women Decide about Work, Career, and Motherhood* (Berkeley: University of California Press, 1985), 7.

19. For work with black mothers see Carol Stack, *All Our Kin* (New York: Harper and Row, 1974); for working class mothers see Lillian Breslow Rubin, *Worlds of Pain: Life in the Working Class Family* (New York: Basic Books, 1976), chapter 5; and Mary Georgina Boulton, *On Being a Mother* (London: Tavistock Publications, 1983).

20. Many significant studies have been done using samples of about thirty. For example, Elizabeth Bott, *Family and Social Network* (London: Tavistock, 1957) used a sample size of twenty families; Daniel Levinson *A Seasons of a Man's Life* (New York: Ballantine Books, 1978) used forty men. More recently, Vangie Bergum, *Woman to Mother: A Transformation* (Massachusetts: Bergin & Garvey, 1989) used a sample of six.

21. Jessie Bernard, *The Female World* (New York: Free Press, 1980), 141-47; Rubin, *Worlds of Pain*, chapter 3.

22. Kenneth Keniston, "Youth: A 'New' Stage of Life," *American Scholar*, Autumn, 1970, uses the term "youth" for this same new period of life.

23. Francine D. Blau & Anne E. Winkler, "Women in the Labor Force: An Overview," in Jo Freeman, *Women: A Feminist Perspective* (Palo Alto, California: Mayfield, 1989), 265-86.

24. Bernard, *The Female World*, 203-7.

25. Joanna Ross and James P. Kahan in "Children by Choice or by Chance: The Perceived Effects of Parity," *Sex Roles*, 1983, 9, 69-77 report that upper-middle class liberal female undergraduates still do not see childfree-by-choice as a positive option. They found that women students projected children as enhancing quality of life for both parents, while men students projected children as lowering life satisfaction.

26. Shirley S. Angrist and Elizabeth M. Almquist, *Careers and Contingencies* (New York: Dunellen, 1975); Mirra Komarovsky, *Women in College: Shaping New Feminine Identities* (New York: Basic Books, 1985), part II.

27. Lydia N. O'Donnell, *The Unheralded Majority: Contemporary Women as Mothers* (Lexington, Mass.: Lexington Books, 1985), 73.

28. Gerson, *Hard Choices*, 7.

29. Robert O. Blood and Donald M. Wolfe, *Husbands and Wives: The Dynamics of Married Living* (Glencoe, Ill.: Free Press, 1960); Sarah Festermaker Berk, "Husbands at Home: Organization of the Husband's Household Day," in Karen Wolk Feinstein, ed., *Working Women and Families*, (Beverly Hills, Calif.: Sage Publications, 1979), 125-58; and Janice M. Steil and Beth A. Turetsky, "Marital Influence Levels and Symptomatology among Wives," in Faye J. Crosby, ed., *Spouse, Parent, Worker: On Gender and Multiple Roles* (New Haven, Conn.: Yale University Press, 1987), 74-90.

30. Jan Pahl, "Patterns of Money Management within Marriage," in Rosenfeld, *Relationships*, 175-97.

31. As reported in Alice H. Cook, *The Working Mother* (Ithaca, N.Y.: Cornell University Press, 1978), 29.

32. Joseph Pleck, "The Work-Family Role System," in R. Kahn-Hut, A. Daniels, & R. Colvard, eds., *Women and Work* (New York: Oxford University Press, 1982), 101-10.

33. Joseph H. Pleck, *Working Wives, Working Husbands* (Newbury Park, Calif.: Sage Publications, 1985), chapter 7.

34. Howe, "The World of Women's Work," 220, points out that, "the When of a woman's work often determines the What," which has negative implications for career development.

35. Bott, *Family and Social Network*, 59-61.

36. Michele Hoffnung, "Teaching About Motherhood: Close Kin and the Transition to Motherhood," *Women's Studies Quarterly*, 1988, XVI, 3 & 4, 48-57.

37. Stack, *All Our Kin*.

38. Pamela Daniels and Kathy Weingarten, *Sooner or Later: The Timing of Parenthood in Adult Lives* (New York: Norton, 1982), 37-8.

39. For fuller discussions of the motherhood mystique and the gap between the expectations and reality of motherhood see Michele Hoffnung, "Motherhood: Contemporary Conflict for Women," in Freeman, *Women*, 157-75, and Louis Genevie & Eva Margolis, *The Motherhood Report* (New York: Macmillan, 1987).

Chapter Two: Alice

1. Ann Oakley, *Women Confined* (Oxford: Martin Robertson & Co., 1980), chapter 8, indicates that first childbirth is a significantly different life event than later ones.

2. Pahl, "Patterns of Money Management Within Marriage," 175-97, refers to this family finance system, in which the wages are given to the wife and the husband is then given an allowance, as the "whole wage system." The other family systems are: "the allowance system," in which the husband gives the wife an allowance out of which she handles some of the family purchases; and "the pooling system," in which all money gets "put in the drawer" and is taken out when needed. The whole wage system assures the wife complete information about financial affairs.

3. Blood and Wolfe, *Husbands and Wives,* chapter 3, point out that keeping track of the finances is tied up with financial decision-making. Both are administrative functions that reinforce each other. In their terms, Alice had a great deal more financial control than most wives.

Chapter Three: Elizabeth

1. Lois M. Verbrugge, "Women's Social Roles and Health," in Phyllis W. Berman and Estelle R. Ramey, eds., *Women: A Developmental Perspective* (Bethesda, Md.: U.S. Department of Health and Human Services, National Institutes of Health, 1982), 58-9, indicates that women with several key roles, such as employment, marriage, and parenthood, are more likely to be healthy than women with few roles. Multiple roles provide more privileges, more resources, and more avenues for self-esteem and social involvement. Women without multiple key roles are more subject to boredom, social isolation, and stress.

Chapter Four: Linda

1. There are only twenty-nine because one of the thirty mothers adopted three children and, therefore, had no pregnancies or births.

2. Reva Rubin, *Maternal Identity and the Maternal Experience* (New York: Springer, 1984) 55, talks about the "loading of knowledge of what to expect" as a normal part of the pregnancy experience. This description did not fit eight of my mothers.

3. All mothers work; childcare and housekeeping are work. Only some are, in addition, employed for wages, usually outside the home.

Chapter Five: Nina

1. Alice S. Rossi, "Transition to Parenthood," *Journal of Marriage and the Family,* 1968, 30, 26-39, analyzes the difficulties of the transition to parenthood and points out some of the factors, like continuing to work, that can ease it.

Chapter Six: Pam

1. Jean A. Ball, *Reactions to Motherhood: The Role of Post-Natal Care* (Cambridge: Cambridge University Press, 1987), p. 145, reports that this reaction is typical of a successful breastfeeder because breastfeeding reinforces the mother's role as the key person in fulfilling her infant's needs.

Chapter Ten: Motherhood Today and Tomorrow

1. Paula Slomin Derry, *Motherhood and the Professional Life: The Case of Women Psychotherapists* (Bristol, Indiana: Wyndham Hall Press, 1990), in a study of professional mothers and non-mothers, found that in anticipation of having their first child the mothers reduced their work hours or changed jobs to reduce their work hours. As a result, after becoming mothers they worked significantly less than the non-mothers.

2. Gray, "The Married Professional Woman" 235-43, found that careful planning of schedules was a coping strategy positively related to satisfaction with work and family roles. See Faye J. Crosby, *Juggling: The Unexpected Advantages of Balancing Career and Home for Women and Their Families* (New York: The Free Press. 1991) for a full discussion of the scheduling and prioritizing that goes into juggling multiple roles.

3. For studies that have focused on differences among women in relation to how much they wanted to have children and had an idealized image of motherhood see: Bernice E. Lott, "Who Wants the Children? Some Relationships among Attitudes towards Children, Parents and the Liberation of Women," *American Psychologist,* 1973, 28, 573-82; Rachel Hare-Mustin and Patricia C. Broderick, "The Myth of Motherhood: A Study of Attitudes towards Motherhood," *Psychology of Women Quarterly,* 1979, 4, 114-28; Mary-Joan Gerson, "The Lure of Motherhood," *Psychology of Women Quarterly,* 1980, 5, 207-18; Mary-Joan Gerson, "Feminism and the Wish for a Child," *Sex Roles,* 1984, 11, 389-99; and Mary-Joan Gerson, "The Prospect of Parenthood for Women and Men," *Psychology of Women Quarterly,* 1986, 10, 49-62.

4. Daniels and Weingarten, *Sooner or Later*, chapter 2, refer to this family-timing scenario as the "natural ideal." They found it to be most common among women who did not go to college.

5. Daniels and Weingarten, *Sooner or Later*, chapter 2, refer to these family-timing scenarios as "pragmatic postponement" and "brief wait." They found that the college-educated women in their sample were evenly divided between these two scenarios.

6. Cynthia Fuchs Epstein, "Multiple Demands and Multiple Roles: The Conditions of Successful Management," in Crosby, *Spouse, Parent, Worker,* 23-35, in her studies of women lawyers found that successful combination of employment, marriage, and parenthood was greatly facilitated by emotional support from significant others, particularly husbands.

7. Two in ten of the mothers without careers worked for pay. In fact, only one third of the mothers had been home continuously since the birth of their first child. In many instances, however, the employment was only a few hours a week, sometimes not regular hours each week. By the standards of labor statistics, the women would have to be considered homemakers rather than workers. And, in many cases, they were overqualified for the jobs they did. Family needs were given priority; employment was fit in around the family's schedule.

8. Bernard Farber, *Family: Organization and Interaction* (San Francisco: Chandler, 1964), 214-15, cites evidence that it is during the childbearing phase that a couple receives the most aid from relatives, usually in the form of home service.

9. Sheila Kitzinger, *Women as Mothers* (Glasgow: William Collins Sons & Co, Ltd., 1978), 120, found, in her study of mothers in many countries, that the pregnant woman in widely different cultures identifies with her mother and becomes closer to her emotionally. Even in the United States, where there has been intense mother-daughter conflict, pregnant daughters gain new understanding of their mothers.

10. At some point, as the parents age, the role reverses and more help is given than received. This process was beginning to happen in the lives of a few of the women but was not yet characteristic of the group.

11. Bott, *Family and Social Network*, 60, points out that close-knit networks result when both husband and wife come into the marriage with close-knit networks and continue to live in the same area after marriage.

12. Eugene Litwak, "Geographical Mobility and Extended Family Cohesion, *American Sociological Review*, 1960, 25, 385-94, stresses that the extended family continues to give aid in spite of geographical mobility which limits face-to-face contact. The aid often comes in the form of presents or money, rather than services, however.

13. Johanna Dobkin Gladieux, "Pregnancy—The Transition to Parenthood: Satisfaction with the Pregnancy Experience as a Function of Sex Role Conceptions, Marital Relationship, and Social Network," in Warren. B. Miller and Lucille F. Newman, eds., *The First Child and Family Formation* (Chapel Hill: Carolina Population Center, 1978), 290-91; and Oakley, *Women Confined*, 153-58, also found that nontraditional women had more conflictual feelings about their pregnancies than traditional ones.

14. Julia A. Sherman, *On the Psychology of Women: A Survey of Empirical Studies* (Springfield, IL: Charles C. Thomas, 1971), chapter 9; and Myra Leifer, "Review Essay: Pregnancy," *Signs*, 1980, 5(4), 756-58, survey research on the physical and emotional effects of pregnancy; Rubin, *Maternal Identity and the Maternal Experience*, analyzes the physical and emotional tasks of pregnancy.

15. Ann Oakley, "A Case of Maternity: Paradigms of Women as Maternity Cases," *Signs*, 1979, 4(4), 607-31; and Barbara Katz Rothman, "Women, Health, and Medicine," in Freeman, *Women*, 81-8, point out how the medical model has been inappropriately applied to pregnancy. As a result research and treatment often approach pregnancy as a sickness rather than a normal state.

16. Another view of pregnancy is that it is a time of psychological well being. While there is some data supporting each interpretation, I believe that the developmental view is more persuasive, gets substantial support from recent work like Rubin, *Maternal Identity and Maternal Experience*, and fits my own data better. On the disagreement, see Leifer, "Review Ar-

ticle: Pregnancy;" Malkah T. Notman, "Pregnancy and Abortion: Implications for Career Development of Professional Women," in Signe Hammer, ed., *Women: Body and Culture* (New York: Harper & Row, 1975), 243-253; and Sherman, *On the Psychology of Women*, chapter 9.

17. Two of the women had had abortions; four had experienced miscarriages.

18. Oakley, *Women Confined*, chapter 8, argues that first childbirth is a significantly different life event than later ones. My own experience and those of my interviewees indicates that the first pregnancy is different as well.

19. At the time of the interviews, only one of these women, Nina, lived in the town where either she or her husband grew up, or where extended family lived, and she came back to her childhood locality already a mother, after thirteen years spent in five different locations including two foreign countries. Although Nina did see her siblings regularly, her mother was dead and she never felt close to her father. She lived two towns away from him and said, "I see my father about three times a year, in a good year two times."

20. Bott, *Family and Social Network*, argues that mobility results in loose-knit social networks which reduces negative sanctions for breaking conjugal role norms.

21. None of the thirty women was devoted to "career first."

22. Of the twenty-seven husband-present deliveries, in fifteen instances the women had peridurals, two demorol, and ten no anesthetic. This compares with the thirty-four husband-absent vaginal deliveries where in fourteen instances women had gas (in twelve of these instances rendering them unconscious), five saddle blocks, nine peridurals, and six no anesthetic.

23. Michael E. Lamb, "Influence of the Child on Marital Quality and Family Interaction During Prenatal, Perinatal and Infancy Periods," in Richard Lerner and Graham Spanier, eds., *Child Influences on Marital and Family Interaction: A Life-Long Perspective* (New York: Academic Press, 1978), 143.

24. Marshall Klaus as cited in Ball, *Reactions to Motherhood*, viii.

25. Ball, *Reactions to Motherhood*.

26. Ann Oakley, *Becoming a Mother* (London: Martin Robertson, 1980), 171 & 323, cites an Office of Population Censuses and Surveys survey which reports that middle-class women are more likely to attend childbirth classes, but I did not find this. It is not clear whether that survey looked at mobility as a factor.

27. Oakley, *Becoming a Mother*, 214, reports, based on her sample of 66 first time mothers, that playing was the favorite paternal task. Changing dirty diapers was the least favored paternal task.

28. Oakley, *Becoming a Mother*, 211, found that one third of her 66 fathers in Great Britain saw their five-month olds for an hour or less a day.

29. Oakley, *Becoming a Mother*, 323, citing the same Office of Population Censuses and Surveys survey, reports that breast-feeding is chosen more often by women from higher social classes. She does not indicate if class background was related to which of her mothers nursed.

30. Sheila Kitzinger, *The Experience of Breastfeeding* (N.Y.: Penguin Books, 1979).

31. Ball, *Reactions to Motherhood*, 145.

32. Sherman, *On the Psychology of Women*, 216, indicates that embarrassment or emotional discomfort can inhibit the letdown reflex so that milk will not flow from a full breast.

33. Fifty-five percent breastfed their babies at least once; 38 percent breastfed at least three months. Myra Leifer, *Psychological Effects of Motherhood: A Study of First Pregnancy* (New York: Praeger, 1980), 99, reports that 25 percent of American women breastfeed, mostly middle-class women, and often for a duration of less than three months.

34. Oakley, *Becoming a Mother*, 171, cites an Office of Population Censuses and Surveys *Infant Feeding* survey that reports more mothers who went to childbirth classes wanted to breast-feed than did non-attenders.

35. Ellen Hock, Karen Christman Morgan, & Michael D. Hock, "Employment Decisions Made by Mothers of Infants," *Psychology of Women Quarterly*, 1985, 9, 383-402, found that career-oriented working mothers differed from non-working mothers in their perceptions of their children's needs. They

were less anxious about separation from their infants and less apprehensive about alternate care.

36. Grace Baruch, Rosalind Barnett, and Carol Rivers, *Lifeprints: New Patterns of Love and Work for Today's Woman* (McGraw Hill, 1983), in a survey of three hundred women, found that control over her work, whether it was paid work or homemaking, was key to a woman's sense of well-being.

Appendix

1. Although the interviews were done over a period of several years, all of the incomes have been adjusted to 1988 dollars using Annual Percent Changes in Earnings and Compensation 1979-1988, U.S. Bureau of the Census, *Statistical Abstract of the United States: 1990*, 110th ed., (Washington, D.C., 1990), 407.

2. Only one woman refused to reveal her husband's income; her embarrassment, their standard of living, and his profession led me to believe it was considerably higher than $82,000.

3. This is the 1988 average annual pay for the NY-NJ-CT Consolidated Metropolitan Statistical Area. *Statistical Abstract*, 408.

4. Donald H. McKinley, *Social Class and Family Life* (New York: Free Press, 1964), 42-3, reviews the literature and presents correlations between various measures of class. He argues strongly that occupational role is the best single indicator and that it is improved very little by adding in additional factors such as education, source of income, amount of income, dwelling area, and house type.

5. Lillian B. Rubin, *Women of a Certain Age: The Midlife Search for Self* (New York: Harper Row, 1979), 215-17, discusses the problems of assigning class status to women. Because of this she looked at the husbands, as well as the women she interviewed, to assess class. I utilized her framework.

6. Eugene Litwak, "Occupational Mobility and Extended Family Cohesion," *American Sociological Review*, 1960, 25, 13, points out that class differences appear to be shrinking, and that the entire occupational structure is becoming more middle

class. This is born out by a comparison of the class status of these women to that of their parents.

7. I define as part-time any work for pay that is less than 30 hours a week.

8. Julia Ericksen, William Yancey, and Eugene Ericksen, "The Division of Family Roles," *Journal of Marriage and the Family*, 1979, 41(2), 306-7, defined a respondent as local if at least two of three specified relatives lived within ten minutes driving distance. These relatives were the closest sibling, the closest grown child, and the parent seen the most often. I could not use the same criteria because only one of my women had grown children. Only two of my local women fail to meet their criteria. One lives near her mother and stepfather, but has no full siblings or grown children. Her father, stepmother, and half-siblings live a few hundred miles away, where she and her mother had also lived until she was fifteen. The other lives where she was raised, as do her four grown siblings, although her parents relocated three years ago.

Further Reading

For the General Reader:

Baruch, Grace, Rosalind Barnett, and Carol Rivers. *Lifeprints: New Patterns of Love and Work for Today's Woman.* (New York: McGraw Hill, 1983). In a survey of three hundred women, the authors found that women need both mastery and pleasure to be satisfied with their lives. This easy to read book examines how marriage, children, and employment contribute to mastery and pleasure.

Burck, Frances Wells. *Mothers Talking: Sharing the Secret.* (New York: St. Martin's Press, 1986). Forty-two vignettes, each a brief personal account focusing on an incident or aspect of a different mother's experience.

Caine, Lynn. *What Did I Do Wrong? Mothers, Children, Guilt.* (New York: Arbor House, 1985). A combination of personal reflection on the author's difficulties raising her two children alone and advice, based on conversations with women and professionals around the country, for mothers who are always asking themselves, "What did I do wrong?"

Chesler, Phyllis. *With Child: A Diary of Motherhood.* (New York: Thomas Y. Crowell, 1979). A moving personal account of a thirty-seven-year-old writer's feelings and conflicts throughout her pregnancy, delivery, and first year of motherhood.

Crosby, Faye J. *Juggling: The Unexpected Advantages of Balancing Career and Home for Women and Their Families.* (New York: The Free Press. 1991). A review of the benefits and costs of multiple roles for mothers, their children, and their men. In addition to showing that the benefits of juggling outweigh the costs, the author provides tips for reducing strain.

Dally, Ann. *Inventing Motherhood: The Consequences of an Ideal* (New York: Schocken Books, 1982). Part I presents an excellent history of motherhood and provides a direct challenge to the standard of exclusive full-time mothering.

Daniels, Pamela, and Kathy Weingarten. *Sooner or Later: The Timing of Parenthood in Adult Lives* (New York: Norton, 1982). A look at how the timing of parenthood affects the quality of the experience, based upon interviews with 86 couples who represent "early," "late," and "very late" first-born children.

Freeman, Jo, ed. *Women: A Feminist Perspective* (Palo Alto, California: Mayfield, 1989). Good introductory essays about many feminist issues, including motherhood, childcare, family and work roles.

Genevie, Louis, and Eva Margolis. *The Motherhood Report* (New York: Macmillan, 1987). Interesting and wide-ranging report on a survey of 870 mothers that richly illuminates the contrast between what women expect of motherhood and the reality they experience.

Gieve, Katherine, ed. *Balancing Acts: On Being a Mother* (London: Virago Press, 1989). Thirteen personal descriptions of the contradictions between motherhood and maintaining a place in the outside world by women with a variety of backgrounds and circumstances.

Kitzinger, Sheila. *The Experience of Breastfeeding* (New York: Penguin Books, 1979). An informative book that addresses all aspects of breastfeeding in a helpful and encouraging way.

Kitzinger, Sheila. *Women as Mothers* (Glasgow: William Collins Sons & Co., Ltd., 1978). A comparative anthropological study of birth and motherhood in different societies and historical periods.

Oakley, Ann. *Becoming a Mother* (London: Martin Robertson, 1980). An exploration of what it means to become a mother, based upon interviews with fifty-five women who delivered their first babies at a particular London hospital.

Roland, Alan, and Barbara Harris, eds. *Career and Motherhood: Struggles for a New Identity* (New York: Human Sciences Press, 1979). Insightful essays about women's struggles to achieve a dual-role identity of career and motherhood, particularly focusing on socio-historical and psychological change.

Rubin, Nancy. *The Mother Mirror: How a Generation of Women Is Changing Motherhood* (New York: G.P. Putnam's Sons, 1984). Examination of the dangers associated with the contemporary maternal styles of either rejecting home-oriented values and following a male pattern, or devoting oneself to home and childbearing when it no longer fits with the economy.

Further Studies:

Ball, Jean A. *Reactions to Motherhood: The Role of Post-Natal Care* (Cambridge, England: Cambridge University Press, 1987). This book, based upon research interviews with 279 English mothers and observations of their midwives and obstetricians, assesses the effects of pregnancy, childbirth, and immediate puerperium on the new mother's adjustment to motherhood and the enjoyment of her infant.

Boulton, Mary Georgina.*On Being a Mother: A Study of Women with Pre-School Children* (London: Tavistock Publications, 1983). Sociological perspectives on women as mothers, based upon interviews with fifty homemakers from a working-class and a middle-class London suburb.

Crosby, Faye J., ed. *Spouse, Parent, Worker: On Gender and Multiple Roles* (New Haven, Conn.: Yale University Press, 1987). Twelve scholarly essays about women's multiple roles, their management, and their consequences.

Derry, Paula Slomin. *Motherhood and the Professional Life: The Case of Women Psychotherapists* (Bristol, Indiana: Wyndham Hall Press, 1990). An academic presentation of the results of an empirical study that compared women psychotherapists who were mothers with those who were nonmothers to see how motherhood affected professional life.

Gerson, Kathleen. *Hard Choices: How Women Decide About Work, Career, and Motherhood* (Berkeley: University of California Press, 1985). A study of sixty-three women between the ages of 25 and 34, from diverse backgrounds, that focuses on their decisions about whether to work or mother.

Leifer, Myra. *Psychological Effects of Motherhood: A Study of First Pregnancy* (New York: Praeger, 1980). A psychological study of nineteen women going through their first pregnancy, delivery, and postpartum, including three case studies of early motherhood.

O'Donnell, Lydia N. *The Unheralded Majority: Contemporary Women as Mothers* (Lexington, Mass.: Lexington Books, 1985). A study of lower- and upper-middle-class mothers focusing on how they frame their commitments to their children, their families, and their communities.

Pleck, Joseph H. *Working Wives, Working Husbands* (Newbury Park, California: Sage Publications, 1985). An evaluation of the division of labor within marriages with working wives, based upon two national studies.

INDEX